COMMUNICATING

···················· Your ····················

COMPETENCE

*A Guide for Non-native Professionals in the
North American Workplace*

BEVERLY B. LEACH

WorldBridges Press
Princeton

For information about permission to reproduce selections from this book, contact
WorldBridges Press, 293 Witherspoon Street, Princeton, New Jersey 08542

www.worldbridgespress.com

Grateful acknowledgement is made for permission to reprint a passage from TED
TALKS, The Official TED Guide to Public Speaking by Chris Anderson, copyright
© 2016 and published by Houghton Mifflin Harcourt, New York.

Library of Congress Control Number: 2017903649.

ISBN: 978-1-4835-9516-0

Leach, Beverly B., 2017

Title: Communicating Your Competence at Work: A Guide for Non-Native
Professionals in the North American Workplace / Beverly B. Leach.

Illustrations by Helen Schrayer

Printed in the United States of America

10 9 8 7 6 5 4 3 2 1

To Owen

for a lifetime of support and encouragement

Contents

Ants shape each other's behavior by exchanging chemicals. We do it by standing in front of each other, peering into each other's eyes, waving our hands and emitting strange sounds from our mouths. Human-to-human communication is a true wonder of the world.

Chris Anderson
Head of TED

What This Book Promises and How to Use It

Some of the brightest, most talented and dedicated professionals in North America today are cultural and geographical newcomers to this part of the world. You may be one of them.

Born and initially educated abroad, you now ply your excellent skills without the benefit of your first language or a culturally comfortable work environment. Within the workplace, the expectations of others –whether a boss, colleagues, team members, clients or an audience—are fraught with confusing signals and sometimes disappointing outcomes.

No matter how proficient you are in your field of knowledge, you may unwittingly deliver unclear messages while trying to convey that knowledge.

This book shows how to communicate your competence so that it will be clearly seen and appreciated by those around you, many of whom may affect –or even determine—your future success.

Whether you are…

- A practicing professional in a scientific or medical field;
- An academic or visiting scholar in a North American university or other research institution;
- Part of a diverse workforce in a global business;
- An ex-pat in North America with management or team responsibilities among locally-born workers; or
- Someone eager to improve professional prospects by finding work or advanced education in North America…

you will learn to take command of your communication by means of clearer pronunciation and verbal delivery, a discrete choice of word expressions, subtle shifts in body language, and an understanding of culturally and situationally appropriate ways of relating to others.

Additionally –and of extreme importance to your professional success—you will learn to present your thoughts and ideas in "the American way." That is, you will construct, frame and order your thoughts so that they are easily and naturally understood by the American mind.

In short, you will learn the "American style of business communication," which directs the conduct of business throughout North America and increasingly in global business settings around the world.

ABOUT THE PREPARATION OF THIS GUIDE

In my 30-year career, I have taught and coached thousands of non-native professionals from more than 80 countries. From my base in Princeton, NJ, I have developed programs to improve the workplace communication of scientists, academics, workers and directors of global businesses operating throughout America. Here now is my summation and synthesis of the most crucial linguistic and cultural challenges to your career success.

Let this be your personal guide, perfected through countless applications to individuals like you. Like others before you, you are likely to discover remarkable improvement and success, for both yourself and for the company or institution you serve.

HOW THE BOOK IS ORGANIZED

Communicating Your Competence moves through eight areas, the result being your ability to perform impressively in meetings and one-on-one's, to deliver a successful presentation and Q & A session, and to forge comfortable relationships with colleagues and clients.

PART ONE – VERBAL COMMUNICATION

Concentrating on verbal clarity, the most obvious, physical aspect of communication

Chapter 1. Fixing Your Accent Where It Matters

Because each native language brings unique challenges to learning English, *your* problems with English pronunciation will be different from those experienced by people from a different background. (What the French can say easily, the Chinese cannot; and what the Chinese find simple, the French do not.) Therefore, Chapter 1 will identify the areas that *you* alone should concentrate on, and not waste time on the problems of others.

Chapter 2. *Your* Troublesome Consonants & Vowels

This chapter concentrates on only those consonant and vowel sounds that are central to the improvement of *your* accent alone. Having identified exactly what you need to work on, you can now streamline your practice for the most efficient use of your time with maximum results. Remember, because *you do not need to master **every** aspect of proper pronunciation in order to speak clearly,* making the right small adjustments can produce huge results.

Chapter 3. Cultivating the "Music" of American English

The third chapter takes verbal communication one important step further, moving you from just "clear pronunciation" to cultivating the more natural-sounding "music" of the language. You will understand how the "American mouth" shapes itself and follows patterns of stress, pacing and downward movement that are unique to a native style of speaking.

PART TWO – NON-VERBAL COMMUNICATION

Using natural American gestures and expressions, creating a "back-and-forth" conversational style, building trust, and framing your ideas for clear, native understanding

Chapter 4. When Gestures Speak Louder Than Words

This chapter explores the subtle, unspoken cues that convey tremendous meaning beyond our words –how we use our eyes, move our head, stand, sit, physically approach a person, make non-verbal utterances (*mmm, ah, uh*), or signal a desire to comment or interrupt. Native speakers understand this instinctively and look for non-verbal indicators when receiving messages. People from other cultures, however, need to learn when and how to use such cues.

This area is relatively easy to master, once you know what to do and have observed it in others. Then, following a "mirroring" technique, you can put your new knowledge into easy practice.

Chapter 5. Connecting with People "American Style"

True competence in the North American workplace requires you to connect with people –whether an audience, colleague or client. Chapter 5 helps you master open "American Style" communication so that others will see you as a worthy team player, brain-stormer, presenter, leader, or generally genial colleague. Whether building comradery and developing trust, or projecting authority and disarming opponents, small but important gestures, along with verbal "lead-in's," can accomplish this with remarkable ease.

Chapter 6. Presenting and Defending Your Ideas

It surprises most people to learn that different cultures (even different countries within the same culture) conceptualize ideas in different ways.

So when you communicate your thoughts to others –whether in writing or speaking—you run the risk of structuring those ideas in a way that can be greatly misunderstood or entirely lost to a listener from another group.

This is a terribly important area to understand and master. You may have the most brilliant breakthrough ideas to the most important, complex problems, but with the wrong delivery structure, your whole point can fail to have the impact it deserves.

PART THREE – THE SUCCESSFUL PRESENTATION

Pulling together all you have learned for a perfect presentation, and then, developing a personal checklist to prepare the ideal talk.

Chapter 7. Pulling It All Together

See how "connecting" is at the core of every element of your presentation. And then from this perspective, you are ready to confidently and clearly present yourself and your message to an audience of any size.

Chapter 8. Your Comprehensive Checklist

This final chapter provides a summary outline reviewing how to integrate every element of a successful presentation. With this detailed overview, you then follow clear steps to building your personal checklist, from the earliest planning stages to rehearsing your final delivery.

So good luck, and have fun transforming your professional life!

PART ONE

Verbal Communication: Reducing Your Accent

1. Fixing Your Accent Where It Matters

2. *Your* Troublesome Consonants & Vowels

3. Cultivating the "Music" of American English

What Might Have Been

Is this happening? After leading my team for six years, the research is ready for FDA review. And who is chosen to present the findings? Mr. NumberTwo in my group, an American of course. And the reason given for this unfair decision? Something about, "Well, Patel, everyone knows it's your baby, but this is too important for anyone to miss a single word." How do I feel? Embarrassed, angry, cheated actually! And longterm, nobody from that important FDA panel will remember me at all.

Chandra Patel,* Ph.D., M.D.

True Confessions

At yesterday's school conference, my daughter's teacher talked the whole time, never stopped to listen to me at all, never tried to understand my concerns.

Sometimes I wonder if anyone knows who I am. I have more than twice the education and responsibility of my child's teacher, my neighbors, or strangers on the phone. Yet it's obvious everyone thinks I sound like just another woman from a foreign country, that I put in routine hours at work every day, that I walk around in a cloud of confusion... unlike them! "Sorry, what did you say?" "I don't really understand what you mean, but let me tell you this..."

And did I mention, my daughter has been correcting my pronunciation since she was four years old!

Magda Krystof,* Microbiologist

Disappointing One's Colleagues

Coming from Indonesia, I re-completed my medical school and residency, and then was lucky to join a large long-established practice.

I was new to the practice, just as three others were, but quickly their patient rosters filled up, while mine never got off the ground. In fact some patients surprised me by asking the front desk to reassign them. They said I was "very polite" but "sometimes didn't seem sure of myself," and anyway they "could not understand me well enough to feel secure" in my care. Is this embarrassing or disheartening? Both, I'd say.

Dr. Ilhan Hartono*

All the frustration, heartache, insecurity and embarrassment expressed by these professionals (*not their real names) could be avoided by taking a few simple steps, for under five minutes a day. Read on!

CHAPTER 1

Fixing Your Accent Where It Matters

Most bright, successful non-native professionals working in North America have already achieved a high measure of English mastery. Grammar is generally at an advanced level, vocabulary is strong (although casual expressions can sometimes trip you up), and writing works best when you stick to formal, more academic expression, and limit the emotional elements.

But then there is the matter of pronunciation. At some point you worked hard to reduce your accent but then allowed your pronunciation to "plateau." You came to accept your accent for what it is, and now in your professional life, you focus on *what* you want to say, not *how* you say it.

American English pronunciation is unforgivingly difficult and often illogical. There are so many different ways to spell a single sound (we, read, need, key, believe, receive, people, machine). Conversely, the same single letter can be pronounced so variously (since, sure, visit, pleasure). The 26 letters of the English alphabet consist of 44 sounds, and among them the five vowels can be pronounced in up to 16 different ways.

But there's good news. None of this needs to be so onerous or impossible. I have simplified it, honed it down to include only those aspects of your speech that you should concentrate on to make the greatest difference in your professional use of language.

This guide will streamline the areas that *you alone* should concentrate on, and not waste time on the problems of others. *You* have different challenges than people whose first language is something else. Simply making the right small adjustments *for you* can produce huge results.

Depending on your first language, this guide gives you just a few individualized critical tips that will require short periods of regular practice for success. You will be working *only* on the few things that matter most for *you,* and let the rest pass.

That leaves time to concentrate on your work, while making dramatic improvements in your speech where it counts.

Your customized program provides help in two areas: first, pointers and practice exercises to deal with your uniquely troublesome consonant or vowel sounds; and then, a primer on cultivating the style and "music" of American English, mastering critical features like pacing, stress, and shaping sounds correctly.

Every practice routine will include:

- From Chapter Two, an all-important set of mouth-control "warmup exercises," tailored to your personal needs. Practice them daily as prescribed, and

    Key sounds that you should work on, with an explanation of how to produce each sound and how to practice it.

By the way, these will generally be consonants, rather than vowel sounds, for one reason. Consonants constitute the framework of language production, whereas vowels are the stylistic embellishment. Consonants are linguistic building blocks, like framing is to a house, without which the building would collapse. But the structure also has details of style, like window design and color, which are comparable to the vowels within words. With this analogy, you can see that consonants make English intelligible, while the vowel sounds account for such things as regional accents.

- And finally from Chapter Three, phrasing, word stress, and pacing, which can often make the biggest difference of all in being clearly understood.

NOW LET'S GET STARTED!

Step #1: From the list below, find your first language in column one, and look across to column two for your "linguistic region" in the world.

Step #2: Find that country or geographic area on the following pages.

Step #3: Read that section to see which elements are especially important to work on.

Step #4: Turn then to the Practice Chart at the end of the section, to get started on your individual practice routine, and forget the rest!

ALBANIAN	Balkan Peninsula
AZERBAIJANI	Caucasus Nations
ARABIC	Arab States
ARMENIAN	Caucasus Nations
BENGALI	Asia, South
BOSNIAN	Balkan Peninsula
BULGARIAN	Balkan Peninsula
BURMESE	Asia, Southeast
CAMBODIAN	Asia, Southeast
CANTONESE	Asia, East (China)
CROATIAN	Balkan Peninsula
CZECH	Europe, Eastern
DANISH	Scandinavia
DUTCH	Europe, Western
ESTONIAN	Baltic Nations (also possibly Russia)

FARSI	Iran
FINNISH	Scandinavia
FRENCH	Europe, Western (France, possibly Africa and Caribbean)
GEORGIAN	Caucasus Nations
GERMAN	Europe, Western (Germany)
GREEK	Greece
HEBREW	Israel
HINDI	Asia, South
HMONG	Asia, Southeast
HUNGARIAN	Europe, Eastern
INDONESIAN	Asia, Southeast
ITALIAN	Europe, Western
JAPANESE	Asia, East (Japan)
KHMER	Asia, Southeast
KYRGYZ	Asia, Central
KOREAN	Asia, East (Korea)
LAO	Asia, Southeast
LATVIAN	Baltic Nations (also possibly Russia)
LITHUANIAN	Baltic Nations (also possibly Russia)
MACEDONIAN	Balkan Peninsula
MALAY	Asia, Southeast
MANDARIN	Asia, East (China and Taiwan)
MONTENEGRIN	Balkan Peninsula
NEPALI	Asia, South
NORWEGIAN	Scandinavia
PERSIAN	Iran and Asia, Central
POLISH	Europe, Eastern

PORTUGUESE	Brazil or Europe, Western (Portugal)
ROMANIAN	Balkan Peninsula
RUSSIAN	Russia
SERBIAN	Balkan Peninsula
SINHALA	Asia, South
SLOVAK	Europe, Eastern
SLOVENE	Europe, Eastern
SPANISH	Latin America possibly Caribbean, and Europe, Western (Spain)
SWAHILI	Africa, Sub-Saharan
SWEDISH	Scandinavia
SWISS German/French/Ital.	Europe, Western (also Germany, France)
TAGALOG	Philippines
TAJIK	Asia, Central
TAMIL	Asia, South
THAI	Asia, Southeast
TIBETAN	Asia, South
TURKISH	Turkey
TURKMEN	Asia, Central
UKRAINIAN	See Russia
URDU	Asia, South
UZBEK	Asia, Central
VIETNAMESE	Asia, Southeast

Based on your first language, find your "linguistic region" here and see in that section the only practice areas you'll need to work on.

1. AFRICA, Sub-Saharan*

This vast region of Sub-Saharan, East and West Africa include more than 50 nations and island states with huge linguistic variety and hundreds of ethnic, tribal and local languages. You may also have fluency in one of several colonial languages, notably French or British English.

Chances are you have studied and already speak the historic colonial language of your country, and so in speaking American English you will carry the accent of that related Western language.

Even if you consider yourself fluent in British English, the African accent's overtones will combine with your British English accent to create a sometimes confusing accent for American listeners. Therefore, the pointers that follow are very important for you.

The most important correction you should make –which applies to all Sub-Saharan African speakers—is the American "R"; second is the "TH." The next area to improve is a command of "Sentence Stress" and "Pacing." Finally, adjusting to a "Forward Mouth Position" will prove very helpful.

Now turn to the Practice Chart on the pages following Region #20 (Turkey). Then check the chart to see which patterns of practice apply to you. Work only in those areas.

*Note: if French is spoken in your region, you should also see "France" under Western Europe for tips to follow there, as well. Or, if Portuguese is spoken in your country, you may want to check Brazil and/or Western Europe also.

2. ARAB STATES

This group includes 22 countries in the Middle East and North Africa where Arabic is spoken.

Arabic speakers have a relatively clear and understandable accent in American English, with the possible exception of the "R," "V" and "W" and a command of proper "Word Stress," "Sentence Stress" and "Pacing." **Now turn to the Practice Chart on the pages following Region #20 (Turkey), check the chart to see which patterns of practice apply to you. Work <u>only</u> in those areas.**

3. ASIA, Central

Central Asia includes the linguistically related countries of Afghanistan, Kyrgyzstan, Tajikistan, Turkmenistan, and Uzbekistan. In addition, in some former Soviet countries, there may be the influence of Russian as well.

To clarify your American English pronunciation, you should work on the consonants "R," "TH," "Sentence Stress" and "Pacing." **Now turn to the Practice Chart on the pages following Region #20 (Turkey), check the chart and see which patterns of practice apply to you. Work <u>only</u> in those areas.** Exception: For those who have studied and spoken Russian for many years, you should also check patterns for Russia.

4. ASIA, East

This group includes China, Japan, Korea, and Taiwan. There are elements in all the languages spoken here that require the same corrections, while there are also a few features unique to one language over the others.

First, for all the languages of East Asia, you should work to correct the "R" and "L," and make significant effort to develop strong tongue muscles required for the English forward-tongue consonants.

In addition, all Chinese languages should work hard on final consonants, especially "T," "D," and "N," another area where proper strong tongue muscles are required.

Korean speakers should add to the above exercises distinguishing "F" and "P," and improving the "TH" and "Z" sounds.

Japanese speakers should add to their list work on the "W," "V," and "SH" sounds.

Now turn to the Practice Chart on the pages following Region #20 (Turkey), check to see which patterns of practice apply to you. Work <u>only</u> in those areas.

5. ASIA, Southeast

Southeast Asia includes the linguistically related countries of Brunei, Cambodia, Indonesia, Laos, Malaysia, Myanmar, Singapore, Thailand, and Vietnam.

Speakers in this region have the same difficulties as those of East Asia –namely, producing an American "R" and "L" and strengthening the tongue muscles required for the forward-tongue consonants -- and in addition, the "TH" and final "V." Some, especially Indonesians, should work on the "SH," as distinct from the "S." All from this region also need to work on stronger diaphragmatic breathing, for a more forceful delivery.

Now turn to the Practice Chart on the pages following Region #20 (Turkey), check to see which patterns of practice apply to you. Work only in those areas.

6. ASIA, South

This vast sub-continental area includes Bangladesh, India, Nepal, Pakistan, Sri Lanka and Tibet. Besides the predominance of Hindi and Urdu, there is also tremendous and beautiful linguistic variety in this region. And one more ingredient in the linguistic mix: with a history of British colonialism throughout, English is still widely spoken.

The fact of widespread spoken English on the sub-continent has a positive effect on the population's command of English grammar and vocabulary, but unfortunately, a negative result in the area of pronunciation. This can produce an unhelpful psychological effect, when you think you know English so well but refuse to admit the limits of your clarity to American listeners.

Americans find you hard to understand because the sound system and speed of your first language is so different from that of English. In particular, the intonation, sentence stress and pacing of your first language is totally different from that of English, so that even if you master all the American English sounds, they can seem incomprehensible to an American listener because of this difference.

Speakers from South Asia need to improve certain consonant sounds –particularly the "V/W" distinction and the "TH"—but also need to work very hard on pacing and downward intonation.

Now turn to the Practice Chart on the pages following Region #20 (Turkey), and check to see which patterns of practice apply to you. Work <u>only</u> in those areas

7. THE BALKAN PENINSULA

This area includes the languages of Albania, Bosnia, Bulgaria, Croatia, Kosovo, Macedonia, Montenegro, Romania, and Serbia. Despite the variations among some of these languages, American English sound production is relatively clear, with the exception of the "R," "TH" and "V/W" distinction. Besides that, only improvement in sentence stress and downward phrasing is needed.

Now turn to the Practice Chart on the pages following Region #20 (Turkey), and check to see which patterns of practice apply to you. Work <u>only</u> in those areas.

8. THE BALTIC

The Baltic Nations of Estonia, Latvia and Lithuania have some accent challenges in common with the Scandinavian countries, as well as an influence from the Russian language.

In particular, you should work on the "TH," "R," and the "V/W" distinction. Also, you should develop a downward intonation and a relaxation of the mouth muscles.

Now turn to the Practice Chart on the pages following Region #20 (Turkey), and check to see which patterns of practice apply to you. Work <u>only</u> in those areas.

9. BRAZIL

The greatest number of Portuguese speakers are from Brazil, Latin America's largest country. Of course the language originated on the European continent, in Portugal. And colonial influences resulted in Portuguese being spoken in the African countries of Angola, Mozambique, Guinea-Bissau, Cape Verde, São Tomé and Príncipe and Equatorial Guinea. With so much geographic breadth, your accent in American English will vary, depending on where your country of origin.

Therefore, Brazilians should pay attention particularly to this section, but also review Western Europe as it applies to Portugal. Everyone else should concentrate on the Western Europe section.

The distinctively "Brazilian" sound relates to the "final L" and "final Y," along with sentence stress and pacing, as you work to move away from a sing-song intonation.

Now turn to the Practice Chart on the pages following Region #20 (Turkey). Then check to see which patterns of practice apply to you. Work only in those areas.

10. THE CAUCASUS

This region includes Armenia, Azerbaijan, Georgia and Southwestern Russia. You will need to concentrate on the American "R," the "TH" and "V-W" distinction. Also, work on slowing down your delivery and relaxing the mouth muscles.

Now turn to the Practice Chart on the pages following Region #20 (Turkey). Then check your linguistic region on the chart to see which patterns of practice apply to you. Work only in those areas.

11. EUROPE, Eastern

Here we include speakers from the Czech Republic, Hungary, Poland, Slovakia and Slovenia. (Linguistically Ukraine is in Section 18 with Russia; Romania is in Section 7, with languages from the Balkan Peninsula.) The two most important consonant corrections for this group are the "TH" and "V-W" distinction. It is true that an accented "R" exists for these speakers, but it is relatively soft and not as distracting as for speakers in other areas of the world. Work instead on sentence stress for overall clarity for impressive results.

Now turn to the Practice Chart on the pages following Region #20 (Turkey). Then check to see which patterns of practice apply to you. Work <u>only</u> in those areas.

12. EUROPE, Western

For purposes of our study, we include in this region Austria, Belgium, France, Germany, Italy, Luxembourg, Netherlands, Portugal, Spain and Switzerland. In addition, you will find sub-groups for speakers from the "Benelux" countries, and then "French," "German," "Italian," "Portuguese," and "Spanish" for speakers of those languages within *and outside* Europe.

In general, Europeans should practice the American "R," "TH," and "V/W" distinction, as well as sentence pacing and stress.

Now refer to the Practice Chart on the pages following Region #20 (Turkey). Then check to see which patterns of practice apply to you. Work <u>only</u> in those areas. However, also check the language sub-groups below to see if there are some areas not needing attention, or others requiring special work.

Benelux Countries and the Netherlands: these countries tend to speak English quite clearly, as do the Scandinavians. You can, therefore, focus on the "TH" and "V/W" distinction, and avoid an upward finish to your sentences. **This group, then, will want to practice the relevant exercises listed on the Practice Chart, and work only in these areas.**

French: the American "R," which poses such problems for most of the non-English-speaking world, is relatively easy for French speakers to correct. So if you are in that category, skip the work on "R." Instead, work twice as hard on the "voiced TH" so as not to confuse it with a "Z" or "T" sound, and practice the "H."

The biggest and most critical challenge for French speakers, though, is remembering to fully pronounce consonants at the end of words. This is important for general understanding, but it also may signal confusion for your listener. For example, if you do not sound a final "s" on a plural subject, your verb will seem grammatically incorrect. (*The* **girls are** *playing outside* will sound like *The* **girl are** *playing outside.*)

Then work on your phrasing, reducing upward sentence intonation and replacing it with a normally downward direction for English. Practice separating your words more, avoiding the French tendency for *liaison*. **French speakers, then, will want to practice the relevant exercises listed on the Practice Chart, and work only in those areas.**

German: Here too, the American "R" is mastered relatively easily for most German speakers, so you may be able to skip that focus. However, work diligently on both the "TH" and the important "V-W" distinction, and then practice sentence flow to remove your tendency to separate words and create a choppy, "impersonal" (to American ears) sound. (This is the opposite of the French *liaison* challenge.) **German speakers, then, will want to practice the relevant exercises listed on the Practice Chart, and work only in those areas.**

Italian: The "V/W" distinction is not a problem for you, but you will need to work on the "TH," "R," and "H" sounds. Very important, too, is the consonant-stop at the end of words, being careful not to connect consonant endings or words in general within a sentence with vowel sounds. **Therefore, practice the relevant exercises listed on the Practice Chart, and work only in those areas.**

Portuguese: You can skip the "V/W" distinction, but do work on the "R" and "TH." Check yourself on final "L," which is a strong problem for Brazilians. Finally, avoid a sing-song phrasing by practicing downward sentence stress.

Portuguese speakers, then, will want to practice the relevant exercises listed on the Practice Chart, and work only in those areas.

Spanish: You can skip the "R" and the "V/W' distinction, but replace it with the important "V-B" distinction. Most important for you is the full expression of consonant sounds at the end of words and eliminating your tendency to separate words with a choppy, halting lack of "flow." Exercises for this are given which will also reduce the Spanish tendency to put an "eh" before opening "S" sounds (*espanish* for *Spanish*). **Spanish speakers, then, should go to the Practice Chart and practice only the relevant exercises.**

13. GREECE

Greece is, of course, a part of Europe, but we list it and a few other countries on the continent separately, because of their unique linguistic features or special affinity with some non-European countries.

Greek is beautiful to listen to and is within the Indo-European family of languages, but Greek speakers struggle with relatively few vowel sounds, namely the American "R" and the "TH." Beyond that, you should move to Part B, working on sentence stress and pacing for a clear overall delivery. **Now turn to the Practice Chart on the pages following Region #20. Then check to see which patterns of practice apply to you. Work <u>only</u> in those areas.**

14. IRAN

With average effort, Farsi speakers can pronounce American English quite clearly. The "R," which is so troublesome to most of the world, is more easily mastered by Persian speakers. Still, check yourself on this consonant, and then continue to work on the "TH" and "V/W" distinctions. After that, concentrate on overall delivery, with word- and sentence-stress and pacing –as explained further in Part B of this chapter-- to make your speech hold the interest of your American listeners. **Now turn to the Practice Chart on the pages following Region #20. Then check to see which patterns of practice apply to you. Work <u>only</u> in those areas.**

15. ISRAEL

Many Israelis speak Hebrew fluently and daily, but may also have the influence of another first language, most commonly these days

Russian. If that is your case, then refer also to that language of origin, too.

Still, speakers of Hebrew will find "R," the "V/W" distinction, "TH" and reducing the "H" sound problematic. Also, refine your understanding of Sentence Stress with its general downward pattern, for effective delivery. **Now turn to the Practice Chart on the pages following Region #20 (Turkey). Then check to see which patterns of practice apply to you. Work only in those areas.**

16. LATIN AMERICA

Here we include Spanish speakers in Mexico, Central America, South America and some islands in the Caribbean. As with Portuguese (see Brazil in Section 9), the versions of Spanish spoken in Latin America and on Europe's Iberian Peninsula (Spain) are distinct enough to create very different accents in American English. Thus, we devote this study routine for the Latin Americans, as follows.

Maybe because Spanish is so widely spoken in North America and because Americans are so used to accommodating the Spanish accent, some Spanish speakers may make less effort to perfect a totally clear American English accent.

You do have important areas to work on, including the American "R," the "TH/D" distinction, the "V/B" distinction, and general practice enunciating fully and clearly consonants at the *ends* of all words.

In addition, the mis-pronunciation of one vowel sound –the "ih"—creates a particularly strong accent-distraction. Spanish speakers tend to pronounce "ih" the same as the "ee" sound, which is one of the strongest elements of the Spanish accent and should be addressed.

As I mentioned earlier, normally pronunciation of vowels is not key to comprehension the way consonants are, but in this case, there are numerous words where confusing certain vowel sounds can cause your listener to misunderstand the word you want to use. You'll see this when practicing the vowel contrast exercises that follow.

And finally, for professional delivery, you should also practice modulating your word and sentence stress and a general downward pattern, to make your speech hold the interest of your American listeners.

Now turn to the Practice Chart on the pages following Region #20 (Turkey). Then check to see which patterns of practice apply to you. Work only in those areas.

17. PHILIPPINES

The Philippines constitute a significant country in Southeast Asia, but linguistically these islands are somewhat distinct, hence this special section.

Both Tagalog and the influence of Spanish on Filipino speakers make it very important to clarify the distinctions between "TH/T," "V/B," and "F/P". In delivery, vocal strength and pitch, along with word- and sentence-stress require practice. **Now turn to the Practice Chart on the pages following Region #20 (Turkey). Then check to see which patterns of practice apply to you. Work only in those areas.**

18. RUSSIA

In addition to Russia and Ukraine, the former Soviet countries of Belarus, Estonia, Latvia, and Lithuania may share some common pronunciation challenges, depending on how much Russian you spoke in your early, formative years.

The Russian and Ukrainian accent in English suffers from a tight, back-of-throat position that makes all sounds seem "harder" than they should be. (Americans use a sort of "slack-jawed," relaxed mouth posture which "stretches out" all vowels and many consonants to make them sound natural to English speakers.)

Correcting this tightness will help you work on the important consonants "R," "TH," and the "V/W" distinction. Also, you have special need to concentrate on a vowel sound, the "ih," which you tend to confuse with the "ee" sound. (As I mentioned earlier, normally pronunciation of vowels is not key to comprehension the way consonants are, but in this case, there are numerous words where confusing this sound can cause your listener to mis-understand the word you want to use.)

And finally, you will want to practice vocal modulation and word- and sentence-stress for improved delivery. **Now turn to the Practice Chart on the pages following Region #20 (Turkey). Then check to see which patterns of practice apply to you. Work only in those areas.**

19. SCANDINAVIA

In general, Danish, Finnish, Norwegian and Swedish speakers all have an impressive command of American English pronunciation and fluency. Still, the "TH" and "V/W" distinctions will probably need work, but beyond that, the most important area to practice is your downward delivery for proper sentence stress. **Now turn to the Practice Chart on the pages following Region #20 (Turkey). Then check to see which patterns of practice apply to you. Work only in those areas.**

20. TURKEY

Even with some accent in American English, Turkish speakers are generally clear and understandable. The most distracting and sometimes confusing sounds are the "TH" (which can sound like a "T" or "D") and the "V/W" distinction. And, as with most other languages, the "R" can always be improved.

Also, Turkish speakers should practice word- and sentence-stress for clear delivery.

Now turn to the Practice Chart on the following pages and see which patterns of practice apply to you. Work only in those areas.

How to Read the Practice Chart

On the following pages is the Practice Chart, listing which areas deserve special attention depending on your first language.

- Find your linguistic region along the first and last vertical columns on the right- and left-hand spread of the chart. Then note which categories are marked for practice along your line.

- The horizontal categories for study begin with certain consonant and vowel sounds, with the pages indicated for each practice. On the right-hand side of the spreadsheet are categories dealing with the "music" of American English. These relate to such things as the degree of muscle tension, flow and connection, emphasis or stress, downward phrasing, and end-strength.

- If nothing is marked in a given area, then skip it. If it is marked with a black dot, then study it. If it is marked by a "circled dot," then that item is optional.

- Within the pages noted for each category listing, everything is explained in detail, with illustrations and daily practice exercises.

NOTE: EVERYONE SHOULD READ, AT LEAST ONCE, THE OPENING PAGES OF BOTH CHAPTERS 2 AND 3, AND THEN GO TO YOUR INDIVIDUALIZED AREAS OF STUDY. This general knowledge provides background for your private practice and will be helpful as you prepare later for presentations or other dialogues in your working life.

AND FINALLY, IN ADDITION TO THE DIRECTIONS FROM THE PRACTICE CHART THAT FOLLOWS, LOOK FOR YOUR LANGUAGE AND REGION IN THE INDEX (AT THE END OF THE BOOK) TO SEE EVERY REFERENCE TO ADJUSTMENTS SUGGESTED FOR YOU.

Practice Chart for "Sounds"

Sounds →	D/T/N	F/P	H	L	R	S/Z	SH	TH	V/B	V/W	ee/ih
study pages:	46-54	54-57	57-60	60-63	63-67	67-72	72-75	76-79	80-83	83-87	87-92
1st Language Region ↓											
Africa/sub-saharan					•			•			
Arab States					•					•	
Asia, Central											
Asia, East											
Chinese	•			•	•	•	•				
Korean		•		•	•	•	•	•	•		
Japanese				•	•		•	•	•	•	•
Asia, Southeast				•	•		•	•		•	
Asia, South								•		•	
Balkan Peninsula					•			•		•	
Baltic					•			•		•	
Brazil					◉			◉			
Caucasus					•			•		•	
Europe, Eastern					◉			•		•	
Europe, Western											
Benelux								•		•	
French			•		◉			•			
German					◉			•		•	
Italian			•		•			•			
Portuguese					•			•			
Spanish					◉				•		
Greece					•			•			
Iran					•			•		•	
Israel			•		•			•		•	
Latin America (except Brazil)					•	•	•	•	•		•
Philippines		•			•				•		
Russia					•			•		•	•
Scandanavia								•		•	
Turkey					◉			•		•	

Practice Chart for "Music"

Mouth Position 95-98	Speed & Flow 100-104	Stress & Emphasis 105-110	Vocal Power 99	Upward & Down Phrasing 110-112	Word Endings 113-114	←"Musical" Elements ← Study pages:
						First Language ↓ Region
•	•	•				Africa/sub-saharan
	•	•				Arab States
	•	•				Asia, Central

						Asia, East
						  Chinese
						  Korean
						  Japanese

			•			Asia, Southeast
	•	•		•		Asia, South
		•		•		Balkan Peninsula
•				•		Baltic
	•	•		•	•	Brazil
•	•					Caucasus
						Europe, Eastern
				•		Europe, Western Benelux
	•	•			•	French
	•	•				German
					•	Italian
				•	•	Portuguese
	•				•	Spanish
	•	•				Greece
	•	•				Iran
		•		•		Israel
				•	•	Latin America (except Brazil)
		•	•			Philippines
•		•				Russia
				•		Scandanavia
		•				Turkey

CHAPTER 2

Your Troublesome Consonants & Vowels

Before We Start:

- The Relationship Between Spelling & Pronunciation
- Understanding "Voiced" and "Unvoiced" Sounds

Included in This Section:

- D, T and N – Upward Curling Tongue Problems
- D and T Confusion
- F and P Confusion
- H
- L
- R
- S and Z
- SH
- TH
- V and B Confusion
- V and W Confusion
- Vowel Sounds: Contrasting "ee" and "ih"

BEFORE WE START: THE RELATIONSHIP BETWEEN SPELLING AND PRONUNCIATION

Spelling is arguably the most inconsistent part of the English language, so how do we understand one another when trying to pronounce the words we see?

Linguists long ago agreed that having a *phonetic alphabet* would be the way to accurately represent the sounds we want to produce. But what they could *not* agree on was *which* system to use. Some even devoted entire careers to developing "a better phonetic alphabet," which now leaves us with a variety to choose from. Some of you may have learned one version, others another, and still others no phonetic alphabet at all—so what can we do?

For our purposes, I have dropped phonetic spelling altogether, and instead will use the basic English alphabet to direct you to the sounds we will be practicing in this guide.

Below are the sounds associated with alphabetic letters. In most cases the pronunciation will be easily understood. In others, like **S** or **SH**, you'll see that spelling alone does not indicate a particular sound. Most of the time (but not always!), when **S** falls within or at the end of a word and follows a vowel or a "voiced consonant," it will be pronounced like "z," (eg: wa**s**, hi**s**, i**s**n't, egg**s**, tomatoe**s**, fall**s**). The **SH** sound in *shell, she and wish*, may also have other spellings, like *ma**ch**ine, licori**c**e and sta**ti**on*.

The American English **TH** –a challenge for most of you-- can at times be "voiced" (that is, engaging the vocal cords or larynx, as with *these, then,* and *the)* or "unvoiced" (meaning that no sound is produced by vibrating and sounding the vocal cords, but only by expelling air, as with *think, three, math*). A phonetic alphabet, would use different symbols for these variants. Here, though, we differentiate by saying either "voiced TH" or "un-voiced TH."

Following are the alphabetic letters indicating sounds you may be practicing, in the order they are presented in the guide.

CONSONANTS

D	like *David, do, different, bed, dungeon, under*
T	like Tom, taste, until, sat, tunnel
N	like *Nick, note, inside, another, bend*
F	like *Frank, fill, telephone, four, half, office*
P	like *Peter, pancake, apple, pinch, people*
H	like *Henry, hundred, his hat, ha-ha, help!*
L	like *Linda, let, lonesome, tall, pulling*
R	like *Ralph, really, rice, terrible, tear*
S	like *Susan, it's, seek, pass, since, century*
Z	like *Zachary, zebra, isn't, was, wizard, thousand*
SH	like *Shelly, Washington, fashion, licorice, station*
TH	like *Theodore, think, three, then, without, father, month*
V	like *Victor, very, average, vanity, vacation, have*
B	like *Bob, benefit, blueberry, habit, babble, bench*
W	like *Wendy, want, when, wish, willow, we*

VOWELS

ee   like *leave, heat, peach, each, steel, green, Tina*

ih   like *live, hit, pitch, itch, still, grin, Tim*

UNDERSTANDING "VOICED" AND "UNVOICED" SOUNDS

Knowing when and how to "voice" a sound, and when and how *not* to "voice," is the key to improving your accent in many areas of English pronunciation, so let's review it now.

You create sound by using your vocal cords in your throat (in your larynx or voice box). When you speak, they vibrate, but when you simply breathe out, they don't. When making a sound to speak, you can put your hands on your throat and feel a vibration, but when simply pushing air out you will feel no vibration.

In many cases in English, certain pairs of consonant sounds are produced exactly the same way in the mouth *except* that one employs voicing, and the other does not. Saying these sounds clearly is often simply a matter of knowing when to "voice" and when not to.

Here's a list of such consonant pairs.

"Voiced" (vocal cords vibrating)	"Un-voiced (air only)
B (bat, big, bill, bull)	**P** (pat, pig, pill, pull)
D (do, down, weed, dim, feed)	**T** (to, town, wheat, Tim, feet)
V (veal, vote, view, of)	**F** (feel, photo, few, off)
G (gut, goal, gill, ghoul)	**K** (cut, coal, kill, cool)
J (Jill, Jew, gin, Jane)	**H** (chill, chew, chin, chain)
S (Sue, singer, bus)	**Z** (zoo, zinger, buzz)
H (short, sure, Confucius),	**ZH** (measure, confusion)
TH (three, thousand, think, thrilling)	**TH** (this, those, the, with)

INDIVIDUAL PRACTICE INSTRUCTIONS
for TROUBLESOME CONSONANTS
and VOWELS

"D," "T," and "N" - Upward Curling Tongue Problems

A weak or incorrect forming of the "D," "T," and "N" sounds is the main feature of most "Asian accents," particularly for Mandarin, Cantonese and Vietnamese speakers.

To say a proper **"D," "T" and "N,"** you must use your tongue in a completely different way than you do in most East and Southeast Asian languages. Your first language either does not have this sound or forms it differently in your mouth. *Therefore, the muscles enabling you to form the sounds correctly for English are very weak and need practice to strengthen them.*

Without this practice, you will not make these sounds strongly and clearly. And these consonants are important and very common in English. Furthermore, it is important in English to sound the **final** consonant in a word strongly and clearly; when these three important consonants fall at the end of words they can be "lost" to the listener.

For these consonant sounds –as well as the "L" discussed later — you must hold your tongue in a concave position and also be able at the same time to raise the tip of your tongue upward to lightly touch the roof of your mouth. We shall work on this until your tongue falls easily but firmly into place.

It is very difficult to position your tongue in a seemingly unnatural way. The best way to start adjusting to this "American tongue position" is with the warm-up exercises prescribed later in this section. But first, let's talk some more about just what this "natural" (for American English speakers) position entails.

What is the Natural American English "Mouth Position"?

The natural resting position for the tongue in English is concave, with the center resting lower than the edges, somewhat like a bowl. When not speaking or using the tongue at all, English speakers tend to let their tongue rest at the bottom of their mouths, but with the tongue tip (the "front edge of that bowl") resting against the back of the lower front teeth.

Because this is in a sense the "default position" for the American English tongue, native speakers have very strong muscles in this area. After all, North Americans have been easing into this position all their lives and are extremely comfortable forming many English consonants that rely on these particular muscles—especially a strong and facile upward tip to the tongue.

Natural Resting Position

FORMING THE "T," "D" and "N"

All three of these sounds are formed the same way in the mouth, using the critically important upward curling tongue tip.

(The only difference among them is how the sound is ultimately voiced). Here's how to form all three:

- Push the *tip* of your tongue against the ridge just above the back of your upper front teeth. The tongue tip will be curled slightly upwards. (To use only the tip, you will touch it quickly and lightly against the teeth; holding it longer and stronger will create instead a flattened end of the tongue, which is not what we want.)

- Then complete sound:

    - For the "**T**," blow only air out of your mouth. Do *not* use the larynx (voice box) in your throat. You should feel no vibration at your throat.

    - For the "**D**" sound, voice the sound in your throat with your larynx. If you touch your throat you should feel a vibration.

    - For the "**N**," you will voice the sound in your throat *and* at the same time blow air out of your nose. "**N**" is one of the few consonant sounds in English that we call "nasal," because the nose is required. If you hold your nose closed, you cannot say "**N**" properly. (That's why, when you have a cold and your nose is congested, air cannot flow properly and your "**N**" is unclear.)

Figure 1 (T-D-N)

THE "UPWARD CURLING TONGUE" WARM-UP EXERCISE

Now, just as you would lift arm weights at the gym (pull-relax, pull-relax, pull-relax), you will shift your mouth into and out of position, like this:

A. Form the American "D" or "T" position*

- Tongue *tip* pushed against the ridge just above the back of your upper front teeth.

- "Voice" the sound with your larynx for the **"D"**; use only air and don't engage the vocal cords for the **"T"**.

B. Say "Duh-Duh-Duh" or "Tuh-Tuh-Tuh". Each time, hold that initial **"D"** or **"T"** with some firmness before moving into the **"uh"** and then releasing.

C. Shift into a relaxed "ah" position.

- Lips open and relaxed, jaw dropped open

- Tongue forward and down, relaxed

- Tongue tip lying on the bottom of the mouth, behind the lower front teeth

D. Say "aaah" (like *father* **or** *mama).*

E. Repeat steps A-D.

If you prefer, you can produce the "N" sound for these exercises, just adding a nasal flow to your voicing. Either way, the important thing is to push your tongue *tip* strongly against the ridge behind your upper teeth. In doing so, *curl that tongue tip up and then push.

And now for your daily practice exercises...

DAILY "UPWARD CURLING TONGUE" PRACTICE EXERCISES

1. **Warm-up Exercises: Do 12 repetitions,** as shown on the previous page.

2. **Now say each sentence below slowly and carefully, preceded by "Duh-Duh-Duh", "Tuh-Tuh-Tuh" or "N-N-N." PAY SPECIAL ATTENTION TO THESE SOUNDS AT THE END OF WORDS and say them fully!**

Say these sentences more slowly than you would in the normal flow of conversation. The object here is to concentrate on each **D, T** or **N** sound as a muscle exercise.

- **Dan** wan**ts** **to** wi**n**.

- Let me **d**onate **t**en **d**ollars **t**o the fu**nd**.

- We wa**nt** **t**o fi**nd** a pave**d** roa**d** to Bos**t**on this af**t**er**n**oon.

- Margare**t** sai**d** she fou**nd** **t**en **d**ifferent ki**nds** of shops **d**own**t**own.

- Whe**n** will the chil**d**ren lear**n** to cou**nt** **t**o **t**en thousa**nd**?

- Se**nd** Ben to Portla**nd** on the afternoo**n** plane.

- Di**d** we consul**t** with Huma**n** Resources abou**t** the pla**n**?

- Fine, let's ge**t** **d**own to business a**nd** **d**efine the problem.

- The **t**rain station is ope**n** **t**wenty-four/seven.

- Can Benjami**n** go **d**own to the beach a**nd** play in the sa**nd**?

- Ca**n** you help **T**o**dd**? Whe**n** will he lear**n** **t**o fe**nd** for himself?

- My son is seven years old this month. On June ninth, in fact.

"D" and "T" CONFUSION

This is a very noticeable accent problem for speakers from Bangladesh, India, Pakistan and Sri Lanka in South Asia, and less so for some Arabic and German speakers.

You probably have a "t" and "d" sound in your first language, but it is produced *differently* from the American version. You will tend to pronounce both letters the same way, while in English the mouth position is slightly different, and the voicing (whether you use the larynx or not) will vary from the "T" (un-voiced) to the "D" (voiced).

Knowing when and how to "voice" a sound, and when and how not to "voice," is the key to improving your accent in this area.

When you study how to form the "T" and "D" sounds below, you'll see that the fundamental difference concerns the issue of "voicing." Influenced by your first language, you will wrongly tend to voice both sounds when speaking English.

At the very beginning of this section (page 43) we discussed voicing, explaining that you create sound by using your vocal cords in your throat (in your larynx or voice box). When you speak, they vibrate, but when you simply breathe out, they don't. When making a sound to speak, you can put your hands on your throat and feel a vibration, but when simply pushing air out you will feel no vibration.

If you do not correct the difference between the American "T" and "D", you will confuse your American listener. Saying the word "to" will sound like "do." Saying "tie" will sound like "die."

Your challenge is to remember not to use any voicing with the American "T." Since you have no problem with the "D" sound, our warm-up and sentence practice will be with the "T" sound only. Concentrating on that should help you to catch yourself when you are tempted to say both "T" and "D" with a voiced sound.

FORMING THE AMERICAN "T"

- Place the *tip* of your tongue behind your upper front teeth, but do not touch the teeth themselves. Instead, touch very *lightly* the ridge just above those upper teeth. Use just the tip. From the "t" sound in your first language, you will tend to push a bit harder, flattening the tip a bit and altering the sound slightly.

- Then take a breath in for a split-second, and then *push* the tongue tip forward, sending the air-sound out **without using any voice in your throat.**

For the American "T" you do not use your voice at all. You are just pushing air out and your vocal cords are not vibrating. If you put your hand on your throat when you say the "T" correctly, you will feel no vibration, sense no movement, and hear no sound. You'll only hear a puff of air.

THE "T" WARM-UP EXERCISE

You should exercise this tongue muscle daily in order to develop a precise and light touch for the American English sound. Practice flicking the tongue tip quickly against the ridge behind the upper teeth –push-relax, push-relax, push-relax—as you say "Tuh-Tuh-Tuh.":

A. Form the American "T" position

- Tongue tip touching lightly the ridge just above the upper front teeth

- While in this position, breathe in slightly

- Push the tongue tip forward forcing air out

B. Say "Tuh." Release. Slowly and carefully repeat "Tuh."

C. Now say "Tuh" twice as fast, 4 times.
   "Tuh-Tuh-Tuh-Tuh."

D. Repeat steps A-C.

And now for your daily practice exercises...

DAILY "T" PRACTICE EXERCISES

1. **Warm-up Exercises: Do 12 repetitions,** as shown above.

2. **Say each sentence carefully, preceded by "Tuh-Tuh-Tuh"**

- T-T-T: Tom ate two pieces of toast.

- T-T-T: To make it spicier, add a touch of Tabasco sauce.

- T-T-T: *I'm* taking a trip to Texas on Tuesday.

- T-T-T: The tiger running loose terrorized the tourists.

- T-T-T: Too little, too late.

- T-T-T: He told a terrible tale to the whole town.

- T-T-T: The tiny tot tumbled down the stairs.

- T-T-T: Please add **t**wo **t**easpoons of honey **t**o my **t**ea.

- T-T-T: **T**winkle, **t**winkle, little star…

- T-T-T: I **t**otally agree. **T**otally.

Note: Initial "T" (at the beginning of words) is the problem, so only they are highlighted. "T" in the middle or ends of words pose no challenge for you and are generally pronounced correctly in American English.

"F" and "P" Confusion

Korean speakers may have special problems differentiating the "F" and "P" sounds in English. For the letter *F* (spelled *F* or *Ph*), they will tend to say "P."

- "office" will sound like "oPPice"

- "physics" will sound like "Pysics"

- "phone" will sound like "Pone"

This confusion is fairly unique to Korean speakers, so Americans are not accustomed to hearing this contrast very often, making the F-P confusion a source of great misunderstanding among native listeners.

"P" is easy for you to say. your lips are closed together, and you then open your lips by shooting out a puff of air: *Puh! Puh!* There is no voicing, no use of the larynx (voice box) to make your throat vibrate.

"F," however, is produced differently. It too is un-voiced, but unlike the "P" sound, "F" uses the upper teeth, as explained below.

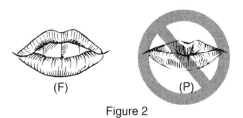

Figure 2

FORMING THE "F"

- Rest your upper front teeth lightly against your lower lip. (Raise your upper lip slightly to get it out of the way of the upper teeth. *If you look in a mirror, you should see the upper teeth.*)

- Blow air through the front of your mouth, around those upper front teeth. Do not use your larynx (voice box) in your throat to vibrate the sound at all. (Vocalizing it in this way will change the "F" into a "V" sound!)

THE "F" WARM-UP EXERCISE

Just as you would lift arm weights at the gym (pull-relax, pull-relax, pull-relax), you will shift your mouth into and out of the "F" position, like this:

A. Form the American "F" position

- Upper front teeth lightly resting on the lower front lip. Upper lip lifted out of the way, revealing the teeth.

- Blow air around those front teeth. Do not voice the sound!

B. **Say "FFF"** Hold that position. Feel your teeth against the lower lip. Look in the mirror and see your teeth –upper lip pulled up toward your wrinkled nose—resembling a snarling dog!

C. **Shift into a relaxed, silent position.**

- Lips open and relaxed, covering the teeth, tongue relaxed, jaw loose. Smile with your lips closed.

D. **Repeat steps A-C.**

And now for your daily practice exercises…

DAILY "F" PRACTICE EXERCISES

1. **Warm-up Exercises: Do 12 repetitions**, as shown on the previous page.

2. **Say each sentence carefully, preceded by "Fuh-Fuh-Fuh"**

    - F-F-F: Frank found some fine footwear at the shoe store.

    - F-F-F: Can you get off the couch and fix the furnace? For sure!

    - F-F-F: Fred is a friendly, fabulous, fantastic fellow.

    - F-F-F: What fantastic flowers!

    - F-F-F: Funny thing, the family didn't feel frustrated about it.

    - F-F-F: Fred, turn off the TV. Your friend Phil is on the phone.

Now let's mix it up with some "P" sounds…

- Don't **fr**y peppers in that **fr**ying pan!

- Please **ph**one me **f**rom Pete's o**ff**ice.

- So**ph**ie and Paul are happy **f**riends.

- He's a patient, e**ff**icient, capable **ph**ysicist.

- **Ph**il, the pilot, **f**lew his plane to **Ph**iladel**ph**ia.

- **F**inally, she put her **f**oot down about **f**ixing the **fr**ont porch!

THE "H" SOUND

Depending on your first language, you may say the American "H" incorrectly so that when you want to say one thing, it will sound like another. The "H" poses a special problem for:

- many French speakers and some Italians, who may not pronounce it at all.

  - *hair* will sound like *air*

  - *hate* will sound like *ate*

  - *I am hungry* may sound like *I am angry.*

- Portuguese speakers, especially those from the north of Brazil, who may substitute "R" or "rr" for "H".

  - *hug* will sound like *rug*

  - *hair* will sound like *rare*

  - *hat* will sound like *rat*

    Americans will say, *He is from **RRRio** or Don't drive your car ("carro") in **RRRecife,*** while many native Brazilians will say *"Hio,"* and Don't drive your *"harro"* in *"Hecife."*

- Hebrew speakers and some Arabic and Russian speakers, who will use a hard, tense voiced sound instead of the lighter, more soft and breathy English "H." American listeners will understand what you're saying, but they will hear a very heavy accent, which you should work to diminish.

Figure 3 (H)

FORMING THE "H"

- Open your mouth wide (as you would when the doctor or dentist ask you to do this).

- Exhale. Give a *strong*, voiceless breath out. Listen for the exhalation sound (just air, no voice) before you say the "H"

- Then flow immediately into the next sound in the word. It will be a vowel sound, which is always voiced. When you express that vowel, you will hear the "H" before it.

THE "H" WARM-UP EXERCISE

In this case, the "H" warm-up is not a muscle building exercise; rather, it is a chance to practice the silent exhalation that precedes a vowel sound, so that it will become more natural and effortless.

A. Form the American "H"

- Mouth wide open. Breathe out strongly, pushing air without any voice.

- With this breath, hear the rush of air only, and then without stopping, move into the next step.

B. **Add "ah"** to the exhalation, and you will hear "Hah." Do this three times, like a good laugh: "ha-ha-ha."

C. **Repeat the exhalation in A above.**

D. **Add other long-vowel sounds (A, E, I, O, U) creating the "H" sound before each one,** so that you will hear "hay" (like *hate*), "hee" (like *he*), "hi" (like *hi, hello!*), "ho" (like *hoe* or *whole*), and "hoo" (like *who*). When you say HAY – HEE – HI – HO – HOO, **be sure to stop between each word to take another breath.**

And now for your daily practice exercises...

DAILY "H" PRACTICE EXERCISES

1. **Warm-up Exercises: Repeat the sequence HAY – HEE – HI – HO - HOO** (as shown in step D on the previous page) **five times. Be sure to stop between each word to take another breath .**

2. **Say each sentence carefully, preceded by exhaling silently first.**

- Exhale: Has Henry ever eaten a hot dog?

- Exhale: Yes, he has. He likes them with hot and spicy mustard.

- Exhale: Harriet has had long hair for half her lifetime.

- Exhale: How does he make himself look so happy all the time?

- Exhale: **He h**as a smile on **h**is face and **h**e's always laughing: **h**a-**h**a!

- Exhale: Why **h**as this **h**orrible meeting gone on so long? I **h**ate meetings!

- Exhale: Are you **h**ungry? Order a **h**amburger like Harry's **h**aving!

- Exhale: **Wh**o wants **h**alf of my **h**amburger? I can't eat the **wh**ole thing.

- Exhale: How does **h**e stay in shape? Healthy **h**abits, that's **h**ow.

- Exhale: I've told you a **h**undred times: wash your **h**ands before you eat!

- Exhale: I've **h**ad **h**ardly anything to eat in the last 24 hours.

- Exhale: Here's **H**arriet's **h**otel. We're meeting **h**er in the lobby.

The "L" Sound

The "L" sound is a particular problem for speakers of many East and Southeast Asian languages. Because you do not have this same sound in your first language, you may not even hear your mis-pronunciation. Americans will notice it immediately, however, so you should work to correct it.

Portuguese speakers from Brazil have problems remembering to form an "L" at the *end* of words. This can be a strong distraction and is the most noticeable element of a Brazilian accent.

A properly pronounced "L" requires you to use your tongue in a way that may not seem natural, so you will need to work hard on building your tongue muscle so that it can move easily and strongly into the "L" position. The best way to do this is with the warm-up exercises prescribed later in this section. These are extremely important to do before using "L" in the sentence exercises.

FORMING THE "L"

Here's how to form the American "L":

- Push the *tip* of your tongue against the back of your upper front teeth or the ridge just above those teeth. The tongue tip will be curled slightly upwards. (Your lips are not shaped in any particular way.)

- Add sound with your larynx (voice box) in your throat, vocalizing "LLLL".

Figure 4 (L)

THE "L" WARM-UP EXERCISE

Just as you would lift arm weights at the gym (pull-relax, pull-relax, pull-relax), you will shift your mouth into and out of the "L" position, like this:

A. Form the American "L" position

- Tongue *tip* pushed against the back of upper front teeth or the ridge just above those teeth.

- "voice" the sound with your larynx

B. Say "LLL" Hold that position with some firmness.

C. Shift into a relaxed "ah" position.

- Lips open and relaxed, jaw dropped open

- Tongue forward and down, relaxed

- Tongue tip lying on the bottom of the mouth, behind the lower front teeth

D. Say "aaah" (like *father* or *mama*).

E. Repeat steps A-D.

And now for your daily practice exercises…

DAILY "L" PRACTICE EXERCISES

1. **Warm-up Exercises: Do 12 repetitions**, as shown on the previous page.

2. **Say each sentence carefully, preceded by "Luh-Luh-Luh"**

- L-L-L: Lions live a long time, but elephants live longer.

- L-L-L: Follow me along the country lane.

- L-L-L: Leonard loves relaxing on lazy days.

- L-L-L: Let me call you later, when I'm leaving school.

- L-L-L: All right, that's a lovely plan.

- L-L-L: Little Lucy was lying on the lawn looking up at the sky.

- L-L-L: Tell me a long story full of colorful details.

- L-L-L: The flower of the Magnolia tree has large, beautiful petals.

- L-L-L: Be careful, William! Lie still; don't move a muscle!

- L-L-L: I'll have a bowl of lentil soup and a small salad for lunch.

- L-L-L: I flew from Philadelphia to Brazil last April.

- L-L-L: Wool socks will help to keep your feet warm in cold weather.

Notes:

- **Asian speakers, be especially careful when words contain both "L" and "R";** don't confuse them! (*Lots of fluffy rice really is terribly difficult to say!*)

- **Brazilian speakers, remember to practice carefully those words with a *final L*.** You will tend to pronounce that L as a W. English speakers will pronounce your country with a clear final L and say *Brazil,* while your Portuguese pronunciation will sound like *Braziw.* You know the proper way to pronounce your own country, but be careful not to carry that pattern to English words. Doing so will create a distracting accent for your North American listeners.

The "R" Sound

It is most difficult to produce a sound if it does not exist in your first language. This is why the American "R" is problematic for almost everyone.

People throughout the world may employ an "R" sound in their own languages variously or not at all. For example, Greeks, South Africans, Russians and Indians –among many others—naturally produce a hard, rolling "R." The French form the sound at the back of their throats with strong tension. Scandinavians and Eastern Europeans generally use a softer, more relaxed but still slightly rolled "r." Chinese, Koreans and Japanese create an "R" that is more like an "L" sound, with the tongue improperly placed. Spanish and Portuguese speakers employ more of a "D" sound.

So almost everyone needs to re-train their mouth muscles so that they can easily fall into the proper American "R" position. The best way to do this is with warm-up exercises, which will be pre-scribed later in this section. These are extremely important to do before going into actual "R" exercises within words.

FORMING THE AMERICAN "R"

Most of you speak with a "rolled R," now. As you do this, you probably lift the tip of your tongue up, curl it slightly back and place it quickly behind your upper front teeth. You then let it touch the front roof area (called the alveolar ridge) once or more. This is very much like the position we assume with the D, discussed on page 48. But for the American "R" you need to change that, because a trilled or "rolled R" does not exist in American English.

Here's what you do to form the American "R":

- Make a round shape with your lips. Your lower jaw will automatically push forward. Feel tension in your lips and let them flare out just a bit.

- Then pull the middle of your tongue high in the back of your mouth. The front of your tongue will stay loose enough to move up and down if you want it to. Instead, though, curl and point the front of your tongue **up,** but **do not let it touch the roof of your mouth.**

- Now to make the "R" sound, try saying "er," but **never, never let your tongue touch anything inside your mouth.** It should just sit there, floating and touching nothing! THAT is the most crucial step, and the most difficult one until you strengthen your tongue muscles through exercise.

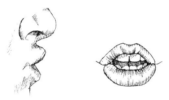

Figure 5 (R – side and front views)

THE "R" WARM-UP EXERCISE

Because the American "R" is such a distinctively unique sound and exists in virtually no other language, everyone of you will have weak, uncoordinated muscles needed for this sound. Strengthening those muscles is therefore of primary importance. Just as you would lift arm weights at the gym (up-down, up-down, up-down), you will benefit from shifting your mouth into and out of the "R" position, like this:

A. Form the American "R" position

- lips rounded, tense, jaw forward

- tongue high and up at the back

- tongue curled upward and FLOATING in the front

B. **Say "er."** Hold the final rrr. No rolling! No tongue touching anything!

C. **Shift into a relaxed "ah" position.**

- Lips open and relaxed, jaw dropped open

- Tongue forward and down, relaxed

- Tongue tip lying on the bottom of the mouth, behind the lower front teeth

D. **Say "aaah"** (like *father* or *mama).*

E. **Repeat steps A-D.**

And now for your daily practice exercises…

DAILY "R" PRACTICE EXERCISES

1. **Warm-up Exercises: Do 12 repetitions**, as shown on the previous page.

2. **Say each sentence carefully and slowly, preceded by "eR-eR-eR."**

- R-R-R: The rain ran off the roof.

- R-R-R: I really like red roses.

- R-R-R: Roy drove his car into the garage.

- R-R-R: Does he prefer to be called *sir* or *mister?*

- R-R-R: Whichever. Either is fine.

- R-R-R: Did you ever hear a cat purr?

- R-R-R: She wears pearl earrings every Thursday.

- R-R-R: That picture is super blurry.

- R-R-R: Don't worry. Eat curry.

- R-R-R: I love my mother, father and my brother Arthur.

- R-R-R: My mother loves warm weather. So does my older sister.

- R-R-R: Hard work is far better than leisure without purpose.

Some of you will have more trouble with "R" at the beginning of a word; others, with the sound in the middle; and still others at the end. Notice what is hardest for you, and practice accordingly.

THE "S" and "Z" SOUNDS

Regardless of your first language, most of you can pronounce "S" clearly and easily.

The problem usually comes when you confuse it with another sound, the "Z." Many language groups may have trouble differentiating the two sounds, so practice is necessary, especially for the "Z" (hint: "S" is un-voiced; "Z" is voiced).

But there is another big problem. **Even if a word is spelled with an "s," it is very often pronounced like "Z"!**

How do you know when to say "S" and when to say "Z"? There is no absolute rule, but here's one tip: **usually if the "S" is preceded by a vowel sound or a voiced consonant, the "s" will be voiced, like "Z." This is the case for many very commonly used words, especially auxiliary verbs, such as** *is (iz), has (haz), was (waz);* **many plural forms or other s-endings like birds (birdz), trees (trEz), plays (plAz), gives (gihvz), says (sehz), etc.**

3. Spanish speakers have another particular problem with "S." When a word **begins** with "S," you will often add the vowel sound "eh" first, making it sound like "eS." For example, instead of saying "Sally wore a skirt to school," you will tend to say *ESally wore **an eskirt** to **eschool**."*

4. And apart from all the above, French speakers have their own distinct challenge: you often confuse "S" *with* "TH." You already know you must work on a proper "TH" so that it doesn't sound like "S." But after you have corrected your "TH" and can say it clearly, you may sometimes even carry it into an actual "S" sound, so that when a "th" is nearby, for example, *thousand* may mistakenly be pronounced *thou-**th**and.*

So let's work on all these problem areas.

FORMING THE "S" is not difficult. To review:

1. Teeth almost touching.

2. Tongue tip sitting just behind (but not touching) the lower front teeth.

3. Air passes through the front teeth, sounding like a hissing snake (s-s-s-s-s).

4. **NO VOICING!** THE THROAT DOES NOT VIBRATE. THE LARYNX (VOICEBOX) IS NOT USED.

Figure 6 (S/Z)

FORMING THE "Z" is exactly the same, but with voicing added, so:

1. Teeth almost touching.

2. Tongue tip sitting just behind (but not touching) the lower front teeth.

3. Air passes through the front teeth, sounding like a hissing snake (s-s-s-s-s).

4. **ADD VOICING.** USE YOUR LARYNX (VOICE BOX) TO ADD SOUND. WHEN YOU TOUCH YOUR THROAT, YOU WILL FEEL VIBRATION.

Now let's go to the daily practice exercises...

CONTRASTING THE "S" WITH "Z"

Warm-up Exercise

A. Form the "S" sound, as just explained, saying it without any throat-voicing. Feel no vibration in your throat.

B. Say S-s-s-s-s, like a hissing snake.

C. Then holding your mouth in the same position, add voicing, making it a "Z."

D. Say Z-z-z-z-z-z. As you do so, feel your throat vibration.

E. Repeat 12 "S-Z" contrasts. SSSSSSS (stop) ZZZZZZZ (stop), etc.

Sentence Practice ("S" sound contrasted with "Z" sound)

Say each sentence carefully and slowly. BE CAREFUL! Even if a word is spelled with an "s," it is very often pronounced like "Z"! There is no absolute rule, but remember, usually if the "s" is preceded by a vowel sound, the "s" will be voiced, like "Z."

First, "S" alone:

- Sally saw Sam at the store.
- Sam said, "So how's it going, Sally?"
- "So-so. I was just going to order something for lunch, maybe soup or a salad.

Then, shifting to "Z":

- She's been working at the zoo for two years.
- And Zack is her husband. Does he work at the zoo too?

- No, he stays home and grows exotic vegetables. Then he prepares amazing salads with them.

Finally, let's see if you can use both sounds together in sentences:

- I was going to buy several pairs of shoes next Tuesday.
- So was I! I need sandals for my trip on Sunday to Arizona.
- I have an easy solution...please, let's go shopping together!
- I was going to propose soup, salad, or a sandwich for lunch.
- Okay then: soup, salad, a sandwich and shoes it is!

NOW SOME SPECIAL "S" PRACTICE FOR SPANISH SPEAKERS (practice saying that!)

To keep from adding an "eh" vowel sound before an *initial* "s," imagine you are starting every "s-word" with a series of s-s-s-s and then go into the word from there.

So, to say *Stella goes to a special school for Spanish speakers,* you would do something like this:

SSSStella goes to a ssspecial sssschool for SSSSpanish sssspeakers.

Practice the following sentences daily, using the above technique:

- *My school is for smart students.*
- *Sports are great. Soccer is my favorite.*
- *Her skirt was several shades of blue.*
- *Spanish sounds so sweet, like music.*

- *Sing me a song in Spanish.*

NOW SOME PRACTICE FOR FRENCH SPEAKERS ONLY:

To remember not to reverse the "S" and "TH" in words that begin with "TH," you need to practice these sentences. With enough repetition, you will become alert to this error and watch for it in daily speech.

- I have a thousand things to do today. I must think positively.

- I'm so thirsty! My throat is as dry as the desert.

- A thirty thousand dollar gift is so thoughtful of you!

- Three things to think about with this airplane: speed, thrust and lift.

- Thread some needles before you start sewing.

THE "SH" SOUND

East and Southeast Asian speakers –Chinese, Korean and Thai in particular—often find this sound difficult to say.

Spanish speakers have a different sort of difficulty with "SH" because they confuse it with the "CH" sound by using their tongue improperly.

FORMING THE "SH"

This sound is formed somewhat like the "S," with the main differences being the tongue and lip position, as follows:

- Your upper and lower teeth will be either touching or almost touching.

- Pull your tongue back, up and away from the front teeth, **and never touching the top of your mouth.** Just let the tongue float in the mouth so that air can rush past it and out of your mouth. (SPANISH SPEAKERS: This is where, if you let your tongue touch the top of your mouth near the front upper teeth, your "SH" will become "CH"!)

- Let the air move out of your mouth, without engaging your voice box.

Start to round your lips, then flare them out slightly, like the bell-end of a trumpet (where the sound comes out of the horn).

Figure 7 (SH)

THE "SH" WARM-UP EXERCISE

This warm-up exercise will contrast the "S" with "SH," a difference most of you should practice, and will help your muscles to shift into and out of this important position.

A. Form the "SH"

- Teeth barely touching or not touching at all.

- Tongue pulled back from the front teeth and floating (touching nothing inside your mouth)

- "Out-round" your lips into a trumpet-like shape

- Let the air move out of your mouth, without using any throat voicing.

B. Now stop, and shift into the "S" position.

- Teeth almost touching

- Tongue just behind the teeth

- Lips are wide (not rounded or "trumpet shaped"), more like a smile.

- Air passes through the front teeth, unvoiced and like a hissing snake.

C. Repeat A and B above, noticing your lips change shape as you do so.

D. Say "sh-sh-she-she-she"; then "s-s-see-see-see" slowly, paying attention to how your mouth parts feel as you shift from one sound to the other.

And now for your daily practice exercises…

DAILY "SH" PRACTICE EXERCISE

1. **Warm-up Exercise: Repeat the sequence "SH"-"S" sequence ("sh-sh-she-she" and "s-s-see-see" ten times, slowly at first and then building speed.**

2. **Practice Sentences:**

   First, try these sentences featuring "SH":

   • *Put the sheets on the shelf.*

- *Shall we share an appetizer of shellfish?*

- *She went shopping for shoes in Chicago*.*

- *Be sure* to shake the bottle before opening it.*

- *Sasha made a fashion statement with her new shoes.*

- *We accept cash only, but there's an ATM machine* outside.*

- *There was a long gash in the metal mesh of the window screen.*

- *Splish-splash, I was taking a bath!*

Now let's mix the "S" and "SH" in the same sentences:

- *The rain shower was so strong that it washed the streets clean.*

- *Susie sold seashells at the seashore.*

- *It was a shocking scene, for sure*.*

- *Hurry up! It sure would be a shame to miss the show.*

- *Honey, you're sweet as sugar*.*

---

* Remember, English spelling is not a certain indicator of correct pronunciation at all! Some common words with "SH" pronunciation will have unusual spelling variations. Examples: *sure, sugar, fuscia, facial, machine, Chicago, passionate, fusion, adhesion,* station, motion, etc.

The "TH" Sound

Most of you will have trouble pronouncing the "TH" sound because it does not exist in your first language. It may even be hard to hear and know whether you are saying it correctly or not.

The "TH" sound in English is sometimes "voiced," as with words like *this* or *the* or *there*. If you don't say it correctly, the "TH" will most often sound like "D" or sometimes "Z" (also voiced sounds).

Or, "TH" can be "un-voiced," as with words like *think* or *thirty* or *through*. In those cases, when said incorrectly the "TH" will most often sound like "T" or sometimes "S" (the un-voiced versions of those same consonant sounds, as shown on page 43).

"Voiced," means you will make the sound by using your larynx (voice box in your throat) while your mouth is in the correct position for this sound. If you put your hand on your throat you will feel a vibration.

For an "un-voiced" sound, you will not use your larynx, but simply blow air out of your mouth while you hold the correct position for this sound. You will feel nothing if you touch your throat in this case.

FORMING "TH"

Your daily practice will start with warm-up exercises to strengthen the mouth parts you'll need for the "TH" sound, and then you will concentrate on forming the actual "TH."

The important mouth parts for this sound are your teeth and the tip of your tongue, as follows:

- Stick out only the *tip* of your tongue from your mouth, and let it rest lightly against the bottom of your top front teeth. If you look in a mirror, you should see a little bit of your tongue between your upper and lower teeth. (If you do not see any tongue, your position is wrong.)

- Then for a "voiced TH," use your larynx to make a humming sound while at the same time keeping your tongue and upper front teeth touching. You will feel your vocal cords vibrate and hear your voice. This is the position for such words as **th**is and **th**e. (Otherwise, they will sound mistakenly like "dis" and "duh," or for French speakers, "zis" and "zee."

- By contrast, for the "un-voiced TH," do not use your larynx to make any sound at all. Simply position the *tip* of your tongue to gently touch the bottom of your upper front teeth, and then blow air through that open space. This is the position for such words as **th**irty and **th**rough. (If you don't position your mouth properly, these words will sound like "tirty" and "troo," or for French speakers, "sirty" and "sroo."

Figure 8 (TH)

THE "TH" WARM-UP EXERCISE

Just as you would do repetitions at the gym (*push-relax, push-relax, push-relax*), you will push your mouth into the "TH" position and then move it back to a neutral, resting pose repeatedly, like this:

A. Form the American "TH" position

- Tongue *tip* forward, *lightly* touching against the bottom of your upper front teeth

- (See or feel the tongue tip protruding outside your mouth)

B. Say "th"

C. Shift into a relaxed silent position.

- Tongue back in your mouth, the front resting behind your bottom teeth

- Lips closed

D. Repeat steps A-C.

These exercises may be done voiced or un-voiced. When you feel comfortable, you can add a degree of difficulty by alternating between creating sound and just blowing air.

And now for your daily practice exercises...

DAILY "TH" PRACTICE EXERCISES

1. Warm-up Exercises: Do 12 repetitions, as shown on the previous page.

2. Say each sentence carefully and slowly.

- I have **th**irty-**th**ree **th**ings to do today. (un-voiced "TH"s)

- **Th**ink a **th**ousand **th**oughts before you speak a single word. (un-voiced)

- It's **th**rilling to **th**row a football **th**irteen yards down the field. (un-voiced)

- Are you **th**rough? Do you **th**ink I'm **th**rough? I **th**ought so. (un-voiced)

- Which of **th**ese do you want, **th**is one or **th**at one? (voiced "TH"s)

- Do you want **th**e burger wi**th** or wi**th**out ketchup? Ei**th**er is fine. (voiced)

- **Th**en it's settled: I'll make **th**is call first and **th**en **th**e o**th**er one. (voiced)

- David's mo**th**er, fa**th**er and bro**th**er live at home wi**th** him. (voiced).

- My bro**th**er Ar**th**ur is **th**irteen but acts like **th**irty. (mixed "TH"s)

- What's the wea**th**er next **Th**ursday? Ei**th**er snow or rain, I **th**ink. (mixed)

- **Th**anks for **th**inking about whe**th**er to go **th**ere alone or wi**th** me. (mixed)

Most of you will have more trouble with the "voiced TH" sounds (saying *the* instead of "duh"), but others –especially South-, Southeast- and East Asian speakers-- will tend to voice everything, so these groups should practice "un-voiced" sounds harder.

"V" and "B" Confusion

This is a problem area for many Spanish speakers, as well as some Japanese, Korean, Filipino, Portuguese, and Southeast Asian speakers.

Like the "F and P Confusion" earlier in this section, exactly the same situation is at work here. In fact, the only difference between the "F and P" grouping and the "V and B" is that the sounds in the first group are un-voiced, while the second group is voiced.

Crucial Note for Spanish Speakers (and others pay attention, too, if this tip is helpful): I like to say that Spanish is a "polite" language (as are some others, like the Southeast Asian languages, for example), inasmuch as the mouth stays fairly closed. No funny faces, no grotesque twists of facial muscles. No wide open mouths, no tongues sticking out, no teeth jutting forward. Just pleasant, soft, discrete attractive smiles.

American English is very different. Everything is "out there," "in your face," visually loud. And while some consonants may be very similar in your first language, in American English you want to "enunciate" or say very clearly every sound –with visual cues (showing the teeth and the tongue at times, opening widely to differentiate vowel sounds, etc.) and prominent vocal sounds (almost spitting, sputtering and blowing).

What this means is that **Spanish and other "discrete" speakers need to move their mouths more, say consonant sounds more strongly, and most important, be sure to *say clearly the sound at the end of every word.***

Now back to the "V" and "B" differentiation. The Spanish speaker will say "very bad," and it will sound to Americans like "berry bad," that is, with no difference heard between the V and the B. The impression on American listeners: a strong, distracting accent.

The "B" sound is easy for you to pronounce. Your lips are closed, and you then open them as you push out a voiced puff of air. That is, as you send sound through your opening lips, you also use the larynx (voice box) to make your throat vibrate.

"V," however, is produced differently. It too is voiced, but unlike the "B" sound, "V" (like the "F") uses the upper teeth, as explained next.

FORMING THE "V"

- Rest your upper front teeth lightly against your lower lip. (Raise your upper lip slightly to get it out of the way of the upper teeth. *If you look in a mirror, you should see the upper teeth.*)

- Blow air through the front of your mouth, around those upper front teeth, and at the same time use your larynx (voice box) in your throat to vibrate the sound.

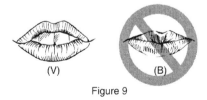

(V)   (B)

Figure 9

THE "V" WARM-UP EXERCISE

Just as you would lift arm weights at the gym (pull-relax, pull-relax, pull-relax), you will shift your mouth into and out of the "V" position, like this:

A. Form the American "V" position

- Upper front teeth lightly resting on the lower front lip. Upper lip lifted out of the way, revealing the teeth.

- Blow air and sound coming from your throat around those front teeth.

B. Say "VVV." Hold that position. Feel your teeth against the lower lip. Look in the mirror and see your teeth – upper lip pulled up toward your wrinkled nose—resembling a snarling dog!

C. Shift into a relaxed, silent position.

- Lips open and relaxed, covering the teeth, tongue relaxed, jaw loose. Smile with your lips closed.

D. Repeat steps A-C.

And now for your daily practice exercises…

DAILY "V" PRACTICE EXERCISES

1. Warm-up Exercises: Do 12 repetitions, as shown on the previous page.

2. Say each sentence carefully, preceded by "Vuh-Vuh-Vuh"

- V-V-V: **V**ictor sent **V**eronica a **v**alentine.

YOUR TROUBLESOME CONSONANTS & VOWELS

- V-V-V: My favorite vest is very valuable.
- V-V-V: Every November the team members have a victory party.
- V-V-V: Vincent voted in the Virginia election.

Now let's combine the "V" and "B" sounds...be careful!

- Victor was a very bad boy.
- November is a very busy month for buying vegetables.
- The best version of the story is my very smart boss Vincent's.
- Vickie likes to wear her best vest with a violet colored blouse.
- Every boy values the ability to play baseball valiantly.
- He's a very big, very brilliant, very athletic boy from Ventura, California.
- Vegetables have lots of vitamins, giving your body vim and vigor!
- Victoria is a very brilliant example of voluptuous beauty.

"V" and "W" Confusion

Your first language may not have a "V" or a "W" sound. Or more commonly, your first language may pronounce our American "V" sound for your alphabet letter "W," and vice versa. Either way, you need to work on the American way of sounding "V" and "W", and not confuse them.

If these sounds do not exist at all in your first language –or as with Japanese or Korean, they are not sounded before certain vowel sounds (*would* and *wool* will sound like "*ood*" and "*ool*"—you must work to strengthen your mouth muscles so that they can more easily fall into the proper American position.

If the "V" and "W" are interchanged, are interchanged, as with Russian, German, some South Asian and many Eastern European languages, you must concentrate on the daily exercises, adjusting your brain and mouth to synchronize the alphabet letter with its proper pronunciation.

If you speak Polish, for example, you must remember when speaking to native North Americans to reverse the sounds in *Olivia and Pavel will wait for you on Wednesday* so that they do not sound like "*Oliwia and Pawel vill vait for you on Vednesday.* You must practice consistently until this becomes automatic.

FORMING THE AMERICAN "V"

This sound is formed with your upper front teeth and your bottom lip. If those two mouth parts are not engaged, your "V" sound will be wrong.

- Touch your upper front teeth against your bottom lip, and hold it there.

- Vibrate your vocal cords in your throat while holding this teeth-lip position.

- Push the sound off your bottom lip and relax.

Figure 10 (V)

FORMING THE AMERICAN "W"

This sound is formed with your lips only. The teeth are not involved at all.

- Round your lips into a circle position, pushing them forward with tension.

- While holding this position, vibrate your vocal cords in your throat.

- Then while still vibrating the sound, release your lips from the circle shape. The sound should stop only after you've relaxed the lips into a more neutral shape.

Figure 11 (W)

THE "V/W" WARM-UP EXERCISE

Just as you would lift arm weights at the gym, you will move your mouth shifting from the "V" to the "W" position like this:

A. Form the American "V" position

- Upper front teeth touching against your bottom lip
- Larynx vibrating

B. **Say "Vuh."** Push the sound off your bottom lip and relax.

C. **Move lips into a rounded position. Feel tension and hold.**

D. **Vibrate vocal cords and continue this sound as you release your lips from their round shape.**

E. **Say "Wuh"** (like "what")

F. **Repeat steps A-E.**

And now for your daily practice exercises…

DAILY "V" and "W" PRACTICE EXERCISES

1. **Warm-up Exercises: Do 12 repetitions**, as shown on the previous page.

2. **Say each sentence carefully and slowly, preceded by "Vuh-Vuh-Vuh-" (Feel your upper teeth touching your bottom lip!)**

   - V-V-V: **V**ictor is **v**ery **v**ain.

   - V-V-V: Thank you **v**ery **v**ery much for the **v**iolets.

   - V-V-V: You should eat a **v**ariety of **v**egetables e**v**ery day.

   - V-V-V: **V**eronica's **v**ision is **v**ery sharp.

   - V-V-V: Can you **v**isualize his **v**alient effort to achie**v**e **v**ictory?

   - V-V-V: Does the e**v**idence **v**erify my **v**ersion of the story?

- W-W-W: What will I wear to the wedding?

- W-W-W: Watch out, or Walter will wander away!

- W-W-W: Will you open the window very wide, or maybe all the way.

- W-W-W: Why won't you learn how to whistle.

- W-W-W: I wish we had won the game.

- W-W-W: Well, well, well…look at that white snow scene outside.

Now let's mix them up (be careful, go slowly)…

- Victor's widow is a very wonderful woman.

- The Wisconsin valley is very wide and wonderfully verdant.

- When will Vicky wear her white shoes?

- We want to leave when I finish making the sandwiches.

- Can you envision a world without violence?

- Every Wednesday I wash the windows and vacuum the rug.

VOWEL SOUNDS: CONTRASTING "ee" AND "ih"

In North American English, our 5 vowels (A-E-I-O-U) are pronounced many different ways, whether alone or in combination. They can all pose a challenge to the non-native speaker. But there is one pair that warrants special attention for virtually everyone: the "ee" versus the "ih" sound.

As I mentioned earlier, the reason we can skip over studying most vowel sounds here is that, while they are important and may be hard to master, vowels are not principally responsible for an unintelligible accent. Consonants are a different story.

Consonants are the essential framework of language production. Say a consonant incorrectly and the word may be mistaken for another with a vastly different meaning. Say a vowel incorrectly and your listener can usually make mental adjustments and understand your meaning. In other words, saying consonants properly makes English intelligible, while vowels are a stylistic embellishment, accounting for such things as regional accents within the United States or Canada. A few words about vowels in general:

> - The five vowel sounds in English –A, E, I, O and U—can have up to 16 different phonetic sounds, some of which will not exist in your first language.
>
> - The differences from one vowel sound to another depend on how you use the jaw, lips, teeth and tongue all together.
>
> - Particularly the tongue will change not only in terms of its shape but also by how far forward or back, and up or down it is in the mouth.

Complicated stuff, so it's lucky we need to discuss only one vowel contrast!

The "ee" and "ih" contrast are particularly important because so many common words exist with these contrasting vowel sounds.

It's easy to confuse meanings in frequently used, similar –but different—sentences, such as:

I'm leaving there now. versus   *I'm living there now.*

Here are a few words that sound very similar but have totally different meanings:

"ee"	"ih"
heat	hit
sheep	ship
sheen	shin
feet	fit
ease	is
sleep	slip
peach	pitch

FORMING THE "ee" (a long vowel...not so difficult)

1. Tongue is in the front of your mouth and high up. *Sides* of tongue rest against sides of upper teeth. Front of tongue touches nothing.

2. Your mouth itself is not open very much.

3. Using your larynx, use voicing, as you do with all vowels.

4. Lips are wide and tense, in a broad, pulled back, smiling shape (BIG smile, teeth showing).

Figure 12 (ee)

FORMING THE "ih" (a short vowel…more difficult)

1. Same as for the "ee" – tongue forward and high. Sides of tongue against sides of upper teeth.

2. Same as for the "ee" – mouth itself not open very much.

3. Same as for the "ee" – sound is voiced in the throat…*BUT!…*

4. **This is where the difference lies: Lips are relaxed (not tense), not as broad a shape, not very pulled back, just a hint of a smile.**

Figure 13 (ih)

Now here are your daily practice exercises…

DAILY PRACTICE EXERCISES - CONTRASTING "ee" and "ih"

Warm-up Exercise (shifting between the "ee" and the "aaah," two sounds at opposite ends of vowel formation positions)

A. Form the "ee" sound, as just explained. Say "ee" while feeling how closed your jaw is and how forward and high your tongue is.

B. Now shift by opening your jaw as wide as you can. Pull your tongue down and back. The teeth touch nothing. Say "aaah, as in *father*.

C. Switch back and forth slowly, in each position feeling how your tongue moves from high-forward to low-back. As you switch, say "ee" – "ee" – "ee" ---- "aah" – "aah" – "aah."

D. Repeat 12 "ee-aah" contrasts.

Sentence Practice ("ee" sound contrasted with "ih" sound)

Say each sentence carefully and slowly. Remember that the only important difference here is that your lips are tense and your smile is broad for the "ee," while lips are relaxed and closed a bit more for the "ih" sound.

- Each week I see Pete.

- We feel extremely keen about eating peaches.

- He'll fit into the family as if he had been here since he was born.

- Sophie and William were sitting in the theater with their cousin Callie.

- Lucy feels ill. Is it her head? Yes, she's dizzy.

- It's a pity we don't have easy answers to the dilemma.

- Sit down and eat your dinner. It's fish with a delicious salad.

- Since the meeting will not interrupt his interview, Steve is happy.

- Philip is investigating the interaction of physics and chemistry.

CHAPTER 3

Cultivating the "Music" of American English

Understandable speech is achieved by clearly articulating the consonant and vowel sounds of American English. But expressing the *music* of the language goes one step further: it gives you the ultimate power to persuade, explain, appeal to, and connect with your listener.

This section will show you how to cultivate a uniquely American style of speaking that will confirm for native listeners how much competence and thorough command of your subject underlie your words.

SPEAKING NATURALLY, "AMERICAN STYLE"

The general speaking style of American English is different from that of your first language. To use a musical analogy, the sounds and speaking patterns of American English are as different from other languages as a waltz is from a tango, a march is from a ballad.

We all have the same mouth parts that enable us to articulate language –the lips and tongue to shape and change sounds quickly, the upper palate for positioning those sounds precisely, the larynx for vocalizing, the lungs for breath and volume, and the jaw for drastic changes in sound formation. But we use those *articulators*, as they're called, in sometimes vastly different ways, and *this* is what accounts for the variety of *linguistic music* worldwide. For example:

- American English is not as rat-a-tat-tat as Spanish, which to Americans sounds rapid-paced and evenly-fired, like a machine gun.

- It does not begin like Chinese with a sudden hard impact and then reverberate by bouncing up or down.

- It is not like French, gargling in the back of the throat, and then with words so connected (or *elided*) that one never hears a break or contrast within a sentence.

- It is not like Russian, with all mouth parts –starting with the throat—tense and tight, and universally sounded high and forward in the mouth.

- It is not like German, punctuated with full stops from word to word, suggesting to American listeners a strong, authoritative, impersonal, sometimes almost threatening tone.

No, American English is easy, relaxed, fluid, lyrical. And like a song, *English glides along with some sounds held longer than others, unevenly paced, moving up at times and usually ending with a downward fall.*

American English is generally relaxed in tone and movement, and fully enunciated with constantly shape-changing lips. This is achieved by attending to five things:

- A Relaxed "American English Mouth"
- Variable Speed, Pacing and Flow of phrases to achieve different aims
- Stress (emphasis) within Words, Sentences & Thought Groups to convey attitude and variable meaning
- Intonation for a natural effect
- Strong Enunciation of Final Consonants for clarity

Let's examine these five key areas, critical for everyone to master successfully.

The Relaxed American English Mouth

Most notably in East and Southeast Asia, but to some degree in dozens of other non-European cultures as well, it is impolite to draw attention to the teeth, lips, or other mouth parts. It can be considered rude to draw attention to the various moving parts of the mouth or to reveal an open mouth. Japanese women, for instance, will politely cover their mouths when they laugh heartily.

Spanish speakers, to a lesser extent, will tend to keep their lips relatively still and in a somewhat smiling shape when they speak. This is why North American listeners are often confused when a

Spanish accent makes the "V" and "B" sound the same in English. Yet inside their mouths the "Spanish tongue" moves more rapidly and evenly than in English, creating a rat-a-tat impression. This also means there is less time to open the mouth widely, which is necessary in English for sufficient lengthening of certain sounds.

In contrast to other languages, in American English everything is open and exposed. It is "out there" for all to see, and in fact this clear view of your mouth helps listeners to understand you!

I have always found it helpful for students to use a mirror when practicing American English sounds, to be sure all the mouth parts used for sound production are doing their respective jobs with a given sound. To practice a proper "TH," for example, you must be able to *see* a bit of your tongue tip extended forward from between your upper and lower teeth.

So for clear American English, you will use your "speech articulators" (the parts of the mouth used for speaking) in this general pattern:

1. **Lips are usually relaxed but active**, moving and changing shape a lot.

   Many languages –particularly Spanish and Asian languages—rely more on the tongue than the lips to create these vocal contrasts. For English, enunciating with your lips serves two purposes: it helps you form the sound precisely and gives your listener a clear *visual* clue about what you're saying.

2. **The tongue will sit low and back in the mouth** when not shaped for a particular sound. This will be the neutral or "default" position when at rest.

Adjusting the tongue position is challenging for speakers of many other first languages. Russian speakers, for example, tend to tense the tongue and hold it high in the mouth.

Chinese, along with other East and Southeast Asian language speakers, find this resting position the biggest challenge. In fact, an incorrect tongue position is responsible for problems saying "R," "L," "T," "D," and "N" clearly. This is because you will naturally rest the tongue in a *convex* shape, whereas in English the tongue should maintain a *concave* shape. This was discussed in detail previously in the Consonants section. But here again is an illustration of that "default" position, with the tongue in its concave, bottom-of-mouth position.

Figure 14
(uh – concave resting position)

You can also feel your tongue moving to the relaxed (aaah) position, down in the mouth, if you practice these contrasting sounds: with your mouth partly open, smile and say EEEEE and then glide directly into AAAAAH. **Keep the rest of your mouth still,** moving only the tongue to feel the strongest contrast.

3. **The jaw will generally be open quite wide**–probably wider than in your first language—unless it needs to be closed for certain sounds (the long EEEE vowel, for example).

   English uses an open jaw frequently because:

   - most of the 16 vowel sounds are articulated with a very open mouth;

   - both syllable stress and word stress –concepts that don't exist in Asian languages—are crucial for clear understanding and require you to stretch out the sound. This is most easily done by opening your jaw wider; and

   - slowing down your speech is helped by opening the mouth wider. And **slowing down should be *everyone's* goal who wants a clear and fluent sound**.

4. **Voice pitch should be deep. For effective American speech, speaking at the lower end of your range, for both men and women, is preferred.**

   Languages will vary as to how deeply they should be spoken. Still, everyone's voice encompasses a range from high to low, even though men's voices are usually lower than women's.

   How high or low you speak may also be a cultural issue. For instance, men in some parts of China and India speak at the higher end of their range. They would sound more authoritative and effective in American business if they dropped their voice pitch lower.

   Women in some cultures –in Japan or Vietnam and sometimes in France, for instance—are encouraged to speak at a higher pitch to sound more feminine. But again, in American culture if one wants to seem confident and authoritative--and this is especially important if you are a woman in business—dropping the voice is one effective solution.

You can achieve this just by lowering your chin closer to your chest when you speak. Pulling your head up and your chin out will *raise* your pitch, which is something you *don't* want to do. So keep your eyes up but your chin down!

5. **Breathe deeply.** Effective American English speech requires strong vocal power. Particularly women in some Asian and African cultures are encouraged to speak softly, but especially women in American business –or anywhere where you want to be taken seriously—should strive to speak strongly in order to appear confident and assertive.

Shallow breathing, from the upper chest, makes you seem childlike and helpless to Americans. Breathing from the diaphragm, deep at the bottom of the lungs, gives you power and authority, which in America is not limited to men.

To breathe deeply, follow the example of opera singers, or Olympic swimmers, or students of yoga: fill your lungs with air to the very bottom of your belly.

When you first inhale, that area should open up. If you place your hand on your belly you can feel it expanding and filling with air. As you exhale, it gradually pulls in, as if your navel were trying to touch your spine, and then the air slowly leaves your upper chest too. If you are breathing incorrectly for English sound production, your *upper* chest will heave up as you take in a breath. This is wrong, and will result in shallow breathing, insufficient for the vocal power needed with American English.

The *Tempo* of American Speech: Its Speed, Pacing and Flow

If you do only one thing to improve your clarity and fluency, it should be to **SLOW DOWN!** This is the single most important piece of advice you will find in this entire guide.

SPEED

Whether you're aware of it or not, you may try to impress others by speaking fast. Or, you may naturally be a fast talker. Or possibly your first language may have an inherent cadence pattern that is *too fast* for American English.

For speakers from the India-Pakistan part of the world, the tempo of your speech is arguably the most critical area for you to work on. Even if you studied English in parallel with your native language since you were a young student growing up, you may be surprised today to hear people say they can't understand you! The problem lies mainly in the multi-syllabic and evenly stressed nature of your first languages that run rapidly and counter to the American English-style stresses that slow speech here in North America.

So whoever you are, wherever you are from, and for this or any other reason, if you pride yourself on speaking rapidly, stop! Instead realize that **the single best way to enhance your impact and to demonstrate your command of clear, fluent American English is by *slowing down* and placing accentuated stresses in the right**

places. This important change can make your speech more persuasive, explanatory, emotional, and just plain clearer.

And there's one more bonus to slowing down. If you have trouble adjusting your mouth to pronounce a particularly difficult consonant sound, by slowing down you have a split-second of extra time to get into position!

PACING

Now let's consider Pacing, which means how you decide *when to vary your speed and how* to do it.

Syllable-timed Languages

Most languages (and probably your first language) are what we call "**syllable**-timed." This means that each syllable –or group of letters containing one vowel *sound* (not vowel *letter*) and usually one or more consonants—receives equal importance and emphasis.

Some Asian languages, like Mandarin, have "single sound words" instead of several syllables in a word, so identifying the number of syllables in an English word may be difficult.

each (1)   care full y (3)   pic ture (2)   in ter es ting (4)

But whether your first language has multiple sound units in a word or not, each of the sound units that you speak will tend to be said with equal importance. In other words, they each receive a separate *but equal* utterance.

Stress-timed Languages

However, English is importantly different. English is "**stress-**timed," meaning that all sound units are not equal. Instead, key syllables in words are "stressed"; that is, they are held longer or said louder than others (***IN** ter es ting in for **MA** tion*).

You will *slow your pace and linger just a little on the stressed syllable*, and then speed up on the unstressed syllables until they are sometimes almost run together. The "stressed syllable" gets the vocal attention.

This *stress-timing* also occurs when we utter a string of words in a full sentence. Here with certain complete words, instead of just syllables, the pace slows and the key elements are held longer and stressed, while other words, like unstressed syllables, are moved through quickly. (This is why we have so many contracted words and shortened utterances in English –*don't* for *do not*, *wanna* for *want to*, *tea 'n' coffee* for *tea and coffee*, etc.; they help us get through the less important words more quickly.)

How, then, do we slow our pace when saying the important words, but speed up with those less content-laden but grammatically necessary words? In one way or another, we sometimes even run them together to move the speaker on to the next important word.

We shall discuss this in detail later in the chapter, but for now remember to think about the words that are key to what you're trying to say, and spend more time on them. To do this you can:

- say those "content words" a little louder (*"will you **please** give me your **attention** for another **minute!**"*), or

- pause just slightly before and after each key word (*"will you...please...give me your...attention...for another...minute!"*), or

- let your voice rise a little in pitch as you say the key words (*"will you PLEase give me your attention for another MINute!"*), or

- vary your pacing by stretching content words out a little longer than the other words (*"will'ya pleeeease gi'me y'r attennnntion f'ranother minnnnute!"*).

Any of these tactics –whichever prove comfortable for you—will help your American listeners hear your important points and will keep them interested in what would otherwise for them be a boring, tedious string of words.

Compare the effect of these two deliveries:

Boring, spoken fast with equal, undistinguished stress:

It-is-important-with-antibiotics-that-you-finish-all-the-pills-in-the-bottle-and-not-stop-just-because-you-are-feeling-a-little-better.

Or now "American style," with pacing –holding onto one word, then speeding through others—to make your utterance easier to grasp:

*It's **important** with **antibiotics** tha'cha finish **all** th'**pills** in th'bottle, an'**not stop** just because you're feelin' a **little better.***

FLOW

Obviously, a drum and a violin do not sound the same. The drum is percussive, sharply distinguishing one sound from the next.

A violin tends to flow, as when the violinist plays a series of notes, fluidly moving one sound into the next.

English is like a violin, not a drum.

We just talked about English being a stress-timed language. But in order for more time to be spent on the stressed words that emphasize the key content of what you want to say, we must move faster through everything else.

While the non-content words may be less important to the meaning of what you want to say, they are still essential to the sentence. They serve the function of holding the sentence together grammatically. They are therefore often called "function" or connecting words. They are spoken quickly, sometimes even run together to move the speaker on to the key "content" words.

How do we "run words together" in English? First, with contractions, second with expressions that shorten several words into one, and third by running the same sound together when it abuts another word with that same sound. (And of course still remember to emphasize the content words.)

You-are-going-to-have-to-stop-pushing-me; it-is-stressing-me-out!

becomes

You're gonna hafta **stoppush**ing me; it's**stressing** me **out**!

The drummer would like the first sentence, but the violinist – and your American listeners—will prefer the second.

The *Dynamics* of American Speech: Emphasizing Key Words Within Sentences & Thought Groups

Syllable-stress Within Words: As a "stress-timed" language, English requires you to apply the principles of emphasis or stress to everything you want to say: your individual words, your sentences, and your larger thoughts that may consist of very long sentences.

Stress works the same in all cases. When you want to say a word correctly, you must know which syllable receives the primary stress and say that word accordingly.

For example, when you want to say the noun "location," you will stress the second syllable lo-**CA**-tion. Yet, the verb "locate" emphasizes a different syllable: **LO**–cate.

So to add stress within a single word, you will say the emphasized syllable

- more clearly,
- slower,
- louder, and/or
- with a slight upward intonation.

This prompts the obvious question: *how do I know which syllable to stress?* As usual in English, there are no absolute rules for which syllable should be stressed in a given word, although you probably have seen or learned some instances where certain patterns usually apply.

For example, *thirty* and *thirteen* (and other such numbers in the "tens" and the "teens") can be easily confused, unless you remember to stress the *first* syllable on the "tens" (**thir**-ty or **fif**-ty) but the *second* syllable for the "teens" (*thir-**teen*** or *fif-**teen**).

Another example: with 2-syllable words that are both nouns and verbs, the noun will be stressed on the first syllable, but the verb will emphasize the second syllable…*Here are your medical **re**cords. Please re**cord** your voice with this microphone. Or, His **con**duct is appalling. How can he con**duct** himself in such a rude manner? Or, Do you wear **make**up all the time, or just for special occasions? Well, I never make **up** my face when I'm alone at home.*

These "rules" are sporadic and subject to exceptions, however, so it's best to look up the phonetic spelling of a word when it truly matters. Also make a habit of listening critically and constantly to native speakers, and then gradually internalize what you hear.

Emphasizing Words Within Sentences:

Varying your speaking is extremely important for everything you do in English, from making presentations, explaining a key point or idea, to simply telling a joke or a story to colleagues.

Always avoid the impression of a tedious and boring monotone by stressing certain words over others. Without variety, your American listeners will "turn you off," and your points will not be clearly heard, understood, or even listened to. **Again like music, vocal delivery in English should be fluid and at the same time punctuated with moments of dynamic strength and interest.**

You'll recall that speakers can stress a word by:

- saying it louder,

- stopping all sound for a split-second before and after the key word,

- raising the pitch of your voice as you reach up to the stressed word, or

- saying the key word very clearly.

Other than wanting to emphasize the most meaningful words in your sentence, is there a general rule for which kinds of words are usually stressed? Yes, "content words" which convey key meaning, can include:

- Nouns (the names of things and persons): ***John, my dog, the microwave, information, chemistry, the street,*** her ***father.***

- Main verbs or action words (but *not* the "helping," auxiliary verbs that form a given tense): he is **eat**ing, have been **wait**ing, doesn't **drive**, has **written**.

- negative words: **no, not, neither, no one, never.**

- question words: **what, whose, when, why, how.**

- some adjectives that describe, when they are important to meaning: **beautiful** girl, **important** advice, **natural** ability, **difficult** project.

- some adverbs, when important (ending in *ly* or otherwise answering the question *where, when, how much, to what extent, how): **neatly, carefully, there, soon, very, easily, fast.***

- any special words needed to convey your special meaning

- the last word in a sentence or phrase: It's all up to **me.**

Conversely, we do *not* generally stress auxiliary verbs (*is, has been, will have*), modals (*can, used to, should, want to, going to*), articles (*a, the*), pronouns (*I, we, them, our*), relative pronouns (*which, that, who*), conjunctions (*and, or, but*), or prepositions (*on, over, for, with*).

Practice stressing the important, "content" words below, and notice why a certain word will receive emphasis or not.

*I've been **trying** to **call** you since **ten** o'**clock**, but you **never answer** the **phone**.*

***When** is your **colleague** going to **arrive**? Is he being **driven directly** to the **hotel**?*

***Where's** your **hat**? I **can't find** it, no matter **where** I **look**.*

*Oh, it's in the **green cabinet**, on the **lower shelf** with the **scarves** and **gloves**.*

Emphasizing Words Within Thought Groups

When writing, it is effective to keep your wording concise, and to mix short, simple sentence forms with complex ones. But in actual speech, we tend to use more words and extend our sentences, in order to express larger ideas.

When speaking, expanded thoughts may exist in one long sentence. But to keep your meaning clear or separate out aspects of the larger idea, speakers will divide the sentence up into various clauses.

Sometimes, in casual speaking, we may tend to run on without thinking about how we might break a long sentence into shorter ones. Instead, in our inattention during conversation, we might say something like this:

> **After he finished work yesterday, Tom walked to the park, where he saw Anita sitting on a bench all by herself reading.**

If we spoke this long complex sentence in a monotone (syllable-timed): *After-he-finished-work-yesterday-Tom-walked-to-the-park-where-he-saw-Anita-sitting-on-a-bench-all-by-herself-reading*), with no breaks or stressed words, it would sound boring or even confusing to North American listeners. As a result, they might lose interest or not follow your thought.

This is why the American English rules for comma placement (different from those of many European countries, as you may know) *use commas to stop the sound momentarily, separate thought groups, and thereby create a clearer sentence.*

Commas are an easy way to add proper vocal stress to thought groups. Of course when you are writing, your commas must be correctly placed, **but for speaking** imagine where you might divide your long sentence into shorter, separate clauses or "thought groups." Then just for a second, stop your voice at the end of each group, and then continue.

For practice, you might create a "vocal script," by dividing the long sentence into shorter groups of words and separate each with visible slash-marks. Then indicate with bold or underlining the key "content" words.

Here's a basic sentence that includes a number of steps of instructions. See where to stop and/or stress your sounds according to the markings.

> *When you **enter** the **building**, // take the **first elevator** on your **right**, // but be sure to **check in** at the **desk first**, // where a uniformed **guard** will **help** you.*

Now try another, and this time if it seems you are too routinely re-starting at each and every clause, group some together into one, to give the sentence more thoughtful shaping.

> *I'd like to **talk** about a **phenomenon** that you've **all observed**, // but it's one which **merits special attention** // when **considering** today's **topic**.*

This is an important pattern. You can practice it when reading even a simple children's book. Or if you are about to deliver a speech or presentation, write your message first, double spaced, and mark the clause endings and strong content words. Then rehearse until you can only quickly gaze down at each thought group before looking up and speaking with an eye to your imaginary audience. From there you will cultivate a natural pattern to gradually adopt whenever you speak at any length.

MOVING UP AND DOWN THE SCALE WITH INTONATION

Intonation is a very important characteristic of fluent North American English. By this I mean the "musical pattern" of a language, as the voice rises or falls in pitch to the higher or lower end of your vocal range while speaking.

- Intonation gives valuable information to your listener. For example, intonation can indicate whether a speaker is finished with a thought and therefore whether you, as the listener, can appropriately enter the conversation.

- It can indicate whether a statement is *giving* information or *asking* for a response.

- In general, proper intonation makes your speech clearer and easier to listen to over extended periods of time.

We've already said that the "music" of English is fluid with moments of dynamic changes within sentences. But along with this is the aspect of intonation. In this realm, English follows a pattern wherein the voice hops up and then steps down.

The Hop Up-then-Step Down Pattern

Notably, the voice does not "slide" up (that would mimic the Scandinavian accent); rather, it "hops" up. Nor does it "roll" down; rather, it "steps" down.

And it does this *only* on your most important words. You can see again how content words in American English can be emphasized through various devices. Intonation is one important technique.

The English intonation pattern is this:

- Hop (don't slide) up to the first important (content) word in a thought group.

- Then step (don't roll) down and land on the next important (content) word.

- Finish your sentence with your strongest step down to the final content word.

Depending on what you want to stress for meaning, some normally key words may be more or less prominent in your pattern. For example, you can say *I can't meet you tomorrow in Dallas* with stronger or weaker intonation of content words, depending on what you want to emphasize.

The voice rises up in pitch to the emphasized word, then drops down to a more even level. Of course you can further emphasize the key word with non-verbal gestures (opening your eyes wider for a moment, using a quick hand gesture, raising your shoulders suddenly, etc.) or vocally by greater volume or holding the word longer.

I can't meet you tomorrow in Dallas. (But my colleague can.)

I **can't** meet you tomorrow in Dallas. (I've already told you, it's impossible.)

I can't **meet** you tomorrow in Dallas. (Not face-to-face, but I could phone you from the airport there.)

I can't meet **you** tomorrow in Dallas. (But I have plans to see your manager that day.)

I can't meet you **tomorrow** in Dallas. (But the next day would work.)

I can't meet you tomorrow in **Dallas**. (Because I'll be in San Francisco then.)

ENDING WITH A STRONG FINISH!

Whenever you say an important word, end a sentence, or finish expressing a meaningful idea, you want to "announce" this by letting the American Style *music* drop down in pitch, and end with strength and clarity.

There's no need to ask yourself which of these (word – sentence – thought group) is the case; just **practice always giving full and clear utterance to the final sound of your final word.**

This is particularly important for speakers of certain first languages whose sounds are uttered with less of a final knockout.

- **Spanish** speakers should work hard on opening up and *saying the consonants at the ends of words very strongly.* You do not naturally move your lips as much as Americans do when speaking, so even though you may *think* you're expressing the final sounds, your American listeners may not hear them at all. The result is confusion and lack of understanding.

  For example, a native speaker asks you, "Are we meeting at four or five o'clock?" And you, the Spanish speaker, might answer, "Fi…." Instead, be sure to follow through to the final "V" sound, holding your mouth in place (upper teeth against the lower lip) for a moment after you think you're finished. Even if you yourself don't hear the full "five," your listeners will when they see your mouth shaped properly in its final position.

- **Chinese** speakers and some others from **East and Southeast Asia** who tend to speak with their mouths discretely closed and lips relatively still, are also very vulnerable to not enunciating final consonant sounds strongly enough. So the same advice given to the Spanish speakers applies to you.

Also, having worked on the "L," "T," "D," and "N" consonants, you now realize that you avoid saying these sounds clearly because they require you to hold your tongue tip *up*, which is an unnatural position in your first language. So practice and become more comfortable with an upward tongue position, and then be sure to form the shape correctly.

If a shoe salesman asks how you like the shoes he's just shown you, be careful not to say, "Dey do.. fi.. we(w)." Instead pay attention to your tongue and hold it in the proper position for each sound that requires the tip to reach upward or touch the upper palate. Then *hold it there* for a split second. Even if you don't hear a difference, your listener will understand your clear response, "**They don't fit well.**"

- And the **French**, whose language silences most final consonants, should pay special attention to the "s" forming noun plurals. Forgetting to express the final "s" will be both confusing and distracting when you seem to pair a singular subject with a plural verb.

"The girl are having a wonderful time" seems grammatically incorrect until you sound fully the final "s" and now we hear, "The girl**s** are having a wonderful time."

Clear English speaking requires you to say the final sound of a word strongly, and the final word of a sentence with the greatest power. If you have softened or dropped altogether the final sound because your mouth has reverted to a shape that is comfortable in your first language, you may notice how soft (or missing!) these final sounds are. But you can be sure that just when you want to make your key point, your American listeners will miss the strong finish you have intended!

My suggestion is that you *over*-emphasize the final consonant sound (at least that's how it will seem to *you*, but American listeners will hear just a natural consonant ending). You can do this either by silently holding your mouth in its final position a split second longer than you feel is necessary, or by adding a slight hint of "uh" after the final consonant sound.

So, in the latter case, "Five plus seven equals twelve" may be expressed:

*Fi-**v**(uh) plu**s**(uh) seve**n**(uh) equal**s**(uh) twel**v**(uh).*

Caution, Italian speakers! Because your first language has a vowel at the end of most words, you will tend to *add* an "uh" to every final consonant. You, then, must do the opposite of what these other speakers are working toward. That is, Italian speakers must be careful not to utter strong "uh" sounds at the end of every consonant. (You don't want *"Give me a break!"* to sound like *"Giv-uh me-uh break-uh!"* Instead, stop yourself at each consonant, creating more silent spaces within sentences. This will give your speech a less sing-song effect. It won't sound as beautiful and operatic as Italian, but it will be more comprehensible in English.

PART TWO

Non-Verbal Communication

Using natural American gestures and expressions;
Creating a "back-and-forth" conversational style; and
Framing your ideas for clear, native understanding.

4. When Gestures speak Louder Than Words

5. Connecting with People "American Style"

6. Presenting and Defending Your Ideas

CHAPTER 4

When Gestures Speak Louder Than Words

I See What You're Saying...

Some may feel this section is superfluous, that you do not need to be taught how to use gestures and body language correctly. And you may be right. But many others will very much need to study this chapter.

Particularly if you are from East and Southeast Asia, or from other hierarchical societies in the world, or if you are female from a stratified society, or if you are a quiet, unassertive personality in general, then this chapter can turn you around and point you directly toward success.

A True Professional Story: Potentially Fatal, Easily Rectified

Li Feng* (*not his real name) explained to me that he thought he had finally "arrived." Every moment of his young adult life had been preparation for this day. Excelling in his native Taiwan's most prestigious university, gaining entrance to Harvard and then MIT, earning two post-doctorates in molecular biology and chemistry, he was now about to enter the American workforce doing important work in his chosen field.

The interviews had gone well. Based on his impressive CV highlighting academic accomplishments, references from highly respected scientists, and papers, dissertations and lab work in ground-breaking areas, HR moved him immediately into discussions with key directors in his field. His English was adequate to talk objectively about his work.

After a 3-week process, young Dr. Li got the news: he would be working for a world-class pharmaceutical company, his first choice, at one of their U.S. locations. He would join a team developing a new drug that could save lives and change the world.

As he walked onto the 8,000 employee campus, he reflected on all this and tried not to get carried away with dreams of his bright future. First he had to get through Day One of his new job.

Corporate life involved more meetings than he'd imagined. He preferred his own research work, but quiet lab time was done best after hours. Still, he was attentive in groups, as he'd always been, mentally noting everything that was said, asking minimal questions. Afterwards he would review the key points and further develop his thoughts on the subject.

He felt comfortable enough with his colleagues, reminding himself of their names and positions, acknowledging them with a nod at meetings or elsewhere in the building.

Imagine his surprise, he admitted to me, when after several weeks his boss called him in for an initial review and expressed concern for how he was adapting. The boss felt he was not attentive at meetings. He did not seem engaged with his colleagues, almost "unfriendly" either from insecurity or feigning superiority. Either way, his teammates viewed him as "unapproachable". As for the work itself, the boss felt Li was either not up to the task ("over his head" was how he put it) or somehow disinterested (his mind was "somewhere else")! Li was uncomfortable as the boss leaned forward and asked, "Is everything all right at home?"

DIAGNOSIS: Everyone was "clueless." Everybody was getting and giving wrong messages.

The team misunderstood Li's involvement, knowledge, interest and desire to work cooperatively.

The boss thought Li was unhappy, distracted by his personal life, not adequately knowledgeable in this complex area, unproductive.

And Li himself believed all was fine!

THE PROBLEM COULD HAVE BEEN EASILY RECTIFIED BY SOME SIMPLE ADJUSTMENTS IN NON-VERBAL EXPRESSION.

When you finish reading this section, test yourself by going to the last page of this chapter to see if you can now identify what Li should have done differently.

I SEE WHAT YOU'RE SAYING...

Sight is the strongest of the five human senses. And so when you communicate, your audience relies greatly on what they *see* as you deliver your message.

Words come out of your mouth and convey some meaning, but how you are *perceived* as you speak can alter that message. And importantly, even when you say *nothing*, you are communicating *something*.

Non-verbal cues communicate a lot of key information about you. How you use your eyes, move your head and facial muscles, stand, sit, physically approach a person, utter non-specific sounds (*mmm, ah, uh*) within conversation, all present clear signals about your competence, your ease in dealing with information, the cooperative give-and-take you exhibit, your willingness to be helpful and non-threatening, and your comfort level in social situations.

This is a subtle process, instinctively understood by native speakers but a confusing challenge for many people from other cultures. In the American workplace you must learn to decipher non-verbal cues, to recognize them in others, and to use them effectively yourself. That is the subject of this section.

OVERALL DEMEANOR

Competent professionals in America are expected to project an image of self-confidence, self-assurance, outward friendliness and knowledgeable control. Their audience –whether clients, colleagues, bosses, whatever—are uncomfortable if you do not disclose these qualities or if you are "hard to read." (Young Dr. Li, at the beginning of this section, thought he was exhibiting all these qualities, but those around him were getting no signals to that effect.)

Your goal should be to seem *relaxed, outgoing, and confident.* You can achieve this in a variety of ways, through:

- Eye Contact
- Facial Gestures
- Body Language
- How You Signal or Interrupt to Enter a Conversation

EYE CONTACT

Making proper eye contact as you speak or listen is critical in American culture. From early childhood, Americans are taught to "look others in the eye" in order to show respect and attention. Deflecting your gaze –as, for example, Asian culture encourages people to do as a sign of respect and deference—in America indicates a lack of connection and personal engagement.

When you are listening to a presentation or lengthy announcements by one person, you should make and hold eye contact with the speaker. You may glance away at times, but always come back to connecting with your eyes.

But when you are *in conversation* with others, or if another person is speaking only briefly and you expect to respond at some point, then you need to be aware of two things.

- First, how long you hold your gaze is key. "Too long" makes you seem to be "staring," which can suggest surprise or confusion, or defiance or threat. "Too short" gives the impression you are nervous ("eyes darting") and unsure of yourself.

  But knowing how long to maintain eye contact is hard to say. Without making this too formulaic, you should make contact, then after about four seconds, divert your gaze for about three seconds, then connect again.

- Second, eye contact is not done in isolation. As you connect, you should *at the same time engage other gestures*, such as facial expressions, nodding and hand gestures, in particular.

FACIAL GESTURES

- **Raising eyebrows** is one way to show either surprise or recognition that something is noteworthy.

- **Smiling** helps to humanize you and make you seem approachable to others. However, men and women smile in different ways; everyone needs to be clear about how to use this gesture appropriately for their gender in a professional setting.

  In American culture, women generally smile more often and more broadly than men. In professional settings women need to control their smiles, interspersing them with flatter, less emotive gestures when thinking or responding to serious issues. That said, professional women sometimes make the mistake of seeming *too* serious, which leaves the impression of being insecure and "trying too hard" to imitate their male counterparts.

Men must remember to open up and smile, just not as effusively as women.

To display a controlled, professional smile, men and women should do so with lips closed, opening the mouth only when greater emotion warrants it. And as with eye contact, shift into and out of that smiling position regularly.

- **Nodding** –that is, moving the head up and down in a slow, relaxed way—conveys your confidence, attention and understanding of what someone is saying. It may also indicate agreement (nodding up and down in American culture also indicates "yes.") Often nodding is done with a subtle smile to show positive, friendly agreement, or with slightly raised eyebrows to signal enthusiastic or firm agreement.

- **"Mutterances"** is my own word for uttering sounds that do not of themselves convey definitive meanings but suggest a sort of vocal gesture. In conjunction with facial gestures "mmmm" emphasizes agreement or thoughtful consideration of what is being said; "aah" suggests you understand ("Oh, I see…") or are surprised to learn something ("Oh, really; that's interesting!"); and "uh-huh" or "mm-hmm" implies that you understand or agree.

BODY LANGUAGE

Remember, your goal is to appear *relaxed, outgoing and confident.* In whatever body pose you assume, you should avoid seeming too tightly self-controlled. Don't look like you are "imprisoned" in your own body space.

Sitting should be natural and not rigid, but at the same time not so relaxed as to seem careless.

- *Legs* should seem comfortable, not placed too precisely parallel to one another. They should not be tightly crossed from hips all the way to the ankles. Nor must both feet be flat on the floor (instead, one heel might be raised against the leg of your chair).

- *Posture* while sitting should be good, back straight or leaning forward from the waist.

- *Arms* should be somewhat expansive, not too close to your body. Avoid tightly crossing your arms, which can create a subconscious barrier between yourself and others.

  You could rest one arm on a table surface or on the arm of your chair. If leaning forward, both elbows could be on the table, perhaps with hands touching one another, fingers loosely knit together.

- *Hands* should be relaxed enough to readily change positions, so that in order to signal your desire to say something, or when you *are* saying something, they are free to move comfortably (but not excessively) to emphasize your comments.

  Avoid folding your hands together and hiding them in your lap below a table surface.

Standing does not require much direction. When someone greets you with the offer of a handshake, you should meet him/her at an equal level by standing up.

Your personal space –that is, the distance you keep from others—is also culturally determined. The Japanese maintain perhaps the greatest "personal bubble" around themselves of any culture, while Mediterranean people naturally crowd close to one another. Americans are somewhere in between these extremes. Again, observe this as you watch those around you, and adapt to what you see.

Touching others is dictated by culture and situation. A general rule to follow in a professional setting is to avoid touching others, except when shaking hands. In the workplace, even casual contact between men and women is discouraged, as corporate policies make very clear. This is particularly so between a man and woman, or a superior with a lower-level worker. One exception to this might be between women colleagues who are also good friends in and outside of work.

Signaling to Enter a Conversation

Signaling –that is, indicating with gestures or in other non-verbal ways—that you want to say something, that you understand, that you don't understand, that you agree, that you disagree, etc. is an important technique to master.

Normally Americans do not stop to ask if everyone understands or wants to add something to the conversation. Americans would commonly expect people to just "jump in" or, as some would put it, "interrupt" when they have something to say.

The American habit of interrupting –that is, cutting off another person's comment in order to interject your own-- is difficult to grasp and to employ, especially for Asian cultures that value silence between words and in conversation, and for women whose cultures say they should defer to men and superiors in general.

Re-training yourself to see interrupting not as rude, but as a cultural practice of *engagement* will take some effort because it runs so against your own native training.

Especially if you feel tentative when talking with fluent English speakers, you need to signal clearly your desire to join the conversation. Signaling helps others to stop and listen, and provides you with a brief space in which to collect your thoughts and then begin to speak.

But how do you signal clearly enough to stop even the most assertive speaker? This is usually done using several gestures or techniques at once.

- Fix your **eyes** on the speaker (forget the "4 second eye contact rule" in this case) and hold them there until you are acknowledged. You might also raise your **eyebrows** slightly to emphasize your concentrated purpose.

- Open your **hands**, lift them or move them forward to draw attention.

- Possibly raise one index **finger** slightly (but do not "point" that finger too strongly).

- Possibly insert your **arm** subtly toward the speaker or into the conversation group.

- **Lean in**, toward the speaker or into the conversation group. Sitting at a table you would bend forward slightly from the **waist** (that is, with your whole upper body, not just your head or chin). Standing, you might slide one **foot** a few inches forward and at the same time shift one **shoulder** in the same direction.

After reading about the non-verbal gestures and techniques in this chapter, you are ready to observe how others employ these traits in real life situations. Make a routine habit of noticing how native speakers in your field and in your part of the country communicate their desires, feelings and competence through non-verbal means.

REGIONAL SUBTLETIES

How strongly you interrupt and how many gestures you use at once will vary, depending on where you live the United States and Canada.

The largest urban centers –particularly New York and through-out the Northeast—have the most intense style of communication. People there talk the loudest, the fastest and most expressively. They interrupt most often, excuse themselves for this least often, and are most direct when expressing opinions.

The American South is the softest-spoken area, with the great-est semblance of politeness –polite expressions, waiting one's turn to talk, consideration of others in a conversation, slower speech, more silences within sentences, softer voice levels.

The Midwest, Southwest, Rocky Mountain West, Pacific Northwest and Canada lie somewhere between the two extremes. People in these areas are open and friendly but not as solicitous as in the super-genteel south.

The next chapter carries this information further. It shows how to integrate your non-verbal image with the actual words you use to join a conversation, answer a question or otherwise leave the impression that you are approachable and interested in those around you.

Returning to the Li Feng Story...

Can you see now what mistakes Li Feng made in the first weeks of his new career?

- *In meetings he should have looked more relaxed, by sitting less stiffly, expanding his arms and upper body more broadly within his space and maintaining eye contact with anyone speaking.*

- *He should have displayed more involvement in the conversation by leaning in at moments when an interesting comment was made or an intriguing idea was posed.*

- *He should have maintained eye contact with the main speaker and others who offered reactions, adding appropriate secondary gestures, like nodding, smiling or momentarily raising his eyebrows.*

- *He should have looked for opportunities to offer comments –brief but substantive—to prove he was a team player. As a new member of the group, his comments should probably have been minimal, but still something. And, to seem confident and relaxed, he should have included some hand and facial gestures to those comments.*

- *If he was unsure about anything, he should have taken the opportunity afterwards to engage with another colleague of equal level to clarify his understanding. This, along with a few more casual comments (see the next chapter for this!)*

would also serve to "break the ice" and begin to forge a friendship.

- Instead of quickly and mechanically nodding as he passed colleagues, he should have looked more directly at them, making eye contact, smiling, and greeting them (by name, if possible).

- If the opportunity presented itself, he might have sought out his boss to offer brief positive feedback about how he felt the job was going so far. At the same time, he should be careful not to appear overly solicitous or too eager to draw constant attention to himself...as Americans would say, he should not appear to be "sucking up" to the boss.

CHAPTER 5

Communicating Your Worth By Connecting with People

Communication is most fundamentally achieved by speaking clearly, and then by adding non-verbal gestures to highlight your intentions in a culturally meaningful way.

But helping others to see *you*, the person behind the voice and gestures, is the true key to success.

Everyone –your boss, your colleagues, your clients, or your audience—must feel a heartfelt connection with you and your message. When this happens, they will respect your knowledge and believe in your ability to accomplish mutual goals.

Sit back, guys, I'll handle this!

At home, at work, and in their dreams at night, Igor Koznetzkov and Boris Gurnofsky (not their real names) were proud men. They each felt they embodied the best of their Russian heritage–their country's superior educational system with its rigorous reliance on scientific method and competitive spirit—and the confidence and intellectual superiority to succeed in America.

They were now well positioned in the same American tech company, poised to produce the next best thing in digital surveillance systems. They spoke rapid English, peppered with colloquialisms, so every American could easily grasp their "inspired" ideas. They believed everyone on the R&D team felt privileged to have Igor and Boris as members.

Brain-storming sessions were fast-paced, even thrilling. At first each member of the development team jockeyed for position as formulator and leader of the next groundbreaking idea. But eventually the Americans would retreat, allowing all the energy to center around Boris and Igor (the brightest lights in the room, as the two men saw it). When the others were silenced and only they were left talking, ideas bounced back and forth like a rapid-fire table tennis match, sometimes with a grand slam finish.

"Listen guys, absolutely my module satisfies all needs," Boris insisted.

"Ridiculous, obviously! Module provides no range," Igor countered.

"You say no range? I say totally acceptable range, easy to prove!"

"So prove, but everyone will see your plan has impossible limitations."

"Impossible? No way, my friend!" Boris tried to get the room behind him, but they all sat in uncomfortable silence.

"By next Monday meeting I will show you clear as bell I am right. No question!" Igor defended himself with a tinge of threat in his voice.

"Well let's not waste more time. We're done here, okay guys?" Boris appeared to close the meeting, as the team looked around in stunned confusion.

DIAGNOSIS:

- Igor and Boris saw each other as worthy sparring partners. They enjoyed showing their American colleagues how the sparks of inspiration flew when bright men exchanged ideas. They interpreted the Americans' retreat as an admission that Igor and Boris had winning ideas and should not be interrupted.

- The Americans were upset and put off by Boris and Igor. They chafed at the Russians' rudeness and direct confrontation. They resented being shut out of the discussion. They wished for momentary reflection of each point raised, before it was so immediately dismissed and replaced by another.

THE RUSSIANS WERE COMPLETELY UNAWARE OF THE IMPRESSION THEY WERE MAKING. COLLEAGUES LABELED THEM "HOPELESSLY INCOMPATIBLE TEAM PLAYERS." THE BOSS SAW THE SITUATION SPIRALING

OUT OF CONTROL AND FELT THEY WERE POISONING THE POSITIVE COMPANY ATMOSPHERE.

The boss and I agreed that Igor and Boris needed to learn how to communicate properly in the American workplace. I gathered a group of ten non-native employees from various countries, including Russia, Greece, Israel and Germany, where a competitive, direct approach was common. We then met for several sessions in a class called "Negotiation and Persuasion Techniques in American Business."

We studied how American-style meetings should flow, how give-and-take is expected, how team involvement at all stages is useful, how politeness fosters a productive exchange of ideas. I explained how clashing cultures can be physically uncomfortable and unproductive, from the initial creative process to the ultimate bottom line. We role-played.

Because of their early mistakes, Igor and Boris lost a lot of career momentum, but at least their new understanding of corporate behavior got them back on track. As you explore this chapter, see how the lessons presented here would have applied to them...and how they should be helpful to you!

Communicating Your Worth by Connecting with People

A productive workplace depends on colleagues getting along well with one another. An effective team requires each member to communicate a sense of cooperation and trustworthiness. A successful business needs its end-users to feel they can count on honesty and openness from their product- or service-provider.

You must learn to communicate your value by showing you can build good relationships, that you are capable of inspiring cooperation and trust, and can be open with others.

In political campaigns, pollsters and strategists try to impress on their candidate-client that *likeability* comes first. Before persuading anyone of anything, the speaker must first create a sympathetic personal connection. Only after this is achieved, can the voter-audience be fully open to hearing the candidate's message and seeing its value.

It's a great compliment to be told, "We speak the same language," in the figurative sense that *we share the same concerns, the same objectives; we're coming from the same place (and I like you for that).*

Good, open communication is all about people *connecting* **with one another.**

We've already seen how spoken words and gestures must be carefully framed and executed so that the speaker and listener understand the same message in the same spirit. In routine daily interactions, you must integrate your verbal expression with your non-verbal signals to reveal something of your personal self.

COMMUNICATING YOUR COMPETENCE

Sometimes because of personality differences, cultural tensions, or just plain misunderstanding through language confusion, problems can arise. Relationships at work can be unpleasant or hold you back professionally. You may find that despite your best efforts, your comradery with Americans may seem to be "stuck," going nowhere.

- As with Igor and Boris, you may seem to be too high energy, in-your-face, direct and confrontational for Americans, and unwittingly push others away;

- or as is common with people from East and Southeast Asia, you may be perceived as too polite and quiet, "not cool or fun," lacking a rapid give-and-take style, and unwittingly leave your listener bored and disinterested.

Either way, the problem is essentially the same: *when communication does not flow between people, the potential for cooperation and respect suffer.* We can fix this by understanding what underlies our differences. Let's consider a simple but common problem, seen in both work and social situations, the matter of *American Small Talk.*

American Small Talk

The most common complaint about American small talk, which you may share, is that it is usually about superficial themes, like the weather ("Great weather we've been having, hmm?"), or subjects that are unfamiliar to "outsiders" ("How about those Yankees yesterday… sweeping the Red Sox!").

The key to dealing with this is: 1) remember that American small talk needs to keep moving, like a ping pong game between two people, following a very clear pattern of give-and-take; and 2) that you can work your way through a topic unfamiliar to you by several means, all with good results.

So in the first instance, how do you keep a conversational ping pong game moving? Follow this simple "hand off" pattern and then see an example of such an exchange:

A's Statement:	Finishes by asking a question or presenting more "leading" information that encourages the other person to add to that topic.
B's Reply:	Answers A's question or offers new information on the subject. Then asks a new question.
A's Reply:	Answers B's question or offers new information on the subject. Then asks a new question.
B's Reply:	Answers A's question or offers new information on the subject. Then asks a new question.

And so forth, until you reach a comfortable moment to close the conversation.

In other words, keep the conversation flowing. Give information with sufficient detail but then move on to ask a related question, showing awareness of your partner and interest in his/her contributions.

In a case where you don't know anything about the subject, you can move the topic along during the "offer new information" phase. Explaining that you don't know much on this theme but are interested gives your conversation partner a chance to interact with you by explaining. Or, you can offer related but different information (I don't know anything about football, but golf is popular in my country) that subtly shifts the subject.

As you find yourself participating more, be careful that you share the talking (remember it's a ping pong game). Monopolizing the conversation dis-connects you from your partner, showing more interest in yourself than in the other person.

And be careful about taboo subjects. Until friendships are very well established, stay away from politics, religion, and intimate personal details.

Here is one example of how a first small talk conversation between "an outgoing American" and "a reticent You" can fall flat, leaving awkward silences and ending with no relationship established.

Small Talk Version #1 – No Connection Communicated

American: *Hi, you're Toji, aren't you?*

You: *Yes.*

American: *Well I'm Frank Henderson, from data development.*

You: *Oh, hello. (Shake hands. Then silence.) Nice party.*

American: *For sure…although, between us, I'd rather be home watching the game.*

You: *What game is that?*

American: *Well, I was thinking the 49ers, although any game would suit me!*

You: *Mmmm.*

American: *Well, listen Toji, nice to see you. Take it easy. (he leaves)*

Diagnosis: One-sided conversation, no energy or engagement offered by You. Very polite but uninteresting to the American. Conversation goes nowhere. Instead, try this corrected version, and see how the dynamics change.

Small Talk Version #2 – Corrected to Keep Interest Flowing

American: *Hi, you're Toji, aren't you?*

You: *Yes, Toji Hatamuro, (you shake hands as you continue), just here two months from Hitachi in Japan.*

American: *Oh wow that must be quite a change...I'm Frank Henderson, from data development. You adjusting okay?*

You: *I'm trying, Frank! We found a nice condo ten minutes from work, so that's convenient for me.*

American: *Sounds great. I have a 30 minute commute, but it's not too bad.*

You: *This is my first company party here. Very nice, isn't it.*

American: *Oh yeah...although between you and me, I'd rather be home watching the game.*

You: *What game? I wish I knew more about American sports.*

American: *Well, I was thinking the 49-ers...that's football, the San Francisco team. I guess baseball is more popular in Japan.*

You: *Yes, and also golf.*

American: *Well you know what, Toji? We have a company softball team starting up next month. I'll let you know the schedule. You can play or watch. Either way, it's a lot of fun.*

You: *That sounds great, Frank. Thanks. I'm glad we talked!*

Diagnosis: The "Question/Answer/Comment/Question" pattern is followed, keeping the conversation flowing. You are giving more than one-word answers. You are revealing yourself enough to open the door for more conversation and more connections. You have left the impression that you are a respectful newcomer but enthusiastic about opportunities to build some level of possible future interaction.

Ping Pong or Basketball?

In the previous example of conversational give-and-take, I referenced "ping pong" as the style to emulate when small-talking. In fact, ping pong is a common metaphor for American-style conversation.

I would qualify that, though, and say yes, ping pong is the style to employ *when **two** persons are talking.* But when you are in a group of several people, ping pong accommodates only two people and leaves the others out, as it involves just a single, direct back-and-forth.

A better metaphor for group conversation would be "basketball." Here, one person leads off with a conversational point. He then "passes the ball" (shifts the talking) to another person, perhaps on his own team (who shares the same point of view). He then enhances the discussion and moves it on. Then the conversation may be interrupted by an opposite team member, who adds something new and turns the conversation in a different direction. He may then either pass it on to a teammate or carry it further, always watching what everyone in the game is doing, in case they want to take a turn. However it goes, everyone feels involved; it's not just a two-way talk.

So, then in a discussion among Anton, Jack, Teresa and Sung:

Anton (going conversationally in one direction): *So we're supposed to devote next Monday to brainstorming and developing a plan and timeline for the project...*

Jack (taking over in the same direction): *Yeah, sounds like a pretty intense day...*

Teresa (adjusting the direction): *Maybe we can make it more fun by meeting somewhere interesting...*

Sung (picking up on that and carrying it forward): *Mmmm...like how about starting at the new campus –there's a conference room there—and then we can break for lunch and go to that new Mongolian Barbeque and Hot Pot place...*

Teresa (starting to reverse direction): *I'm a vegetarian, remember. Barbeque doesn't do it for me...*

Sung (taking the ball back in her direction): *No, they have great vegetarian hot pot selections; you'll love it...*

Jack (carrying the ball all the way to the basket): *I love the idea of getting out of here. I say let's do it!* (all the while looking around him and sensing by their non-verbal gestures a consensus) *Okay then!* **(Slam dunk!)**

Beware of Silence - Keep the Flow Going

Cultural linguists generally agree on this notable fact: Americans are uncomfortable with silence, which leads us to the *Unspoken Rule about Keeping the Flow Going.*

Depending on your first culture, this may be completely antithetical to all you have been taught about conducting a polite, respectful conversation. You will need to understand this cultural difference in order to both adjust your conversational style and not be offended by what you might perceive as American rudeness.

When there is a lapse in the conversation, Americans will feel the need to fill the void, to say something, anything! Especially in business areas, a smooth conversationalist will keep the flow going. Business people may not add much content to the conversation, but they will add easy "lead-in's" and re-phrasing to avoid an awkward pause ("well, I'm sure you've got a point there, but remember, as I said before, the important thing is to...").

In academic and scientific circles, silent, thoughtful moments may be more acceptable, but even there, verbal embellishment may be made. People might, for example, mention the thought process that underlies the silence ("hmmm, so maybe this deserves more careful consideration, and what I'm thinking is...").

So what are some of these useful phrases? That will depend on the situation and the occasion. More on this as you read further, but best for now is to observe how native speakers fill the silent moments, both verbally and through gestures and non-verbal expressions. Make this an ongoing practice and when you can, try to "mirror" their gestures and responses.

Likewise, successfully concluding an interaction involves the same gradual "verbal fadeout," too. Instead of a curt, one-word "okay," you might adjust this abrupt termination with, for example, "okay, sounds good. I'll go back and work on that!"

Polite Conversation, American Style

Politeness is relative; what impresses people in one culture can offend in another. This is an important distinction to understand if you want to be taken seriously and viewed respectfully by your colleagues.

In America, the usual norm is:	In Your Culture?
Not allowing too much silence into conversation.	???
Interrupting (but politely. Americans would call this "enthusiastic interaction"), rather than waiting for permission or another blatant indicator that it's your turn to speak.	???
Speaking directly (but politely), rather than holding back your opinion.	???
Disagreeing within a conversation, rather than waiting to be asked your opinion or expressing it long afterwards.	???
Explaining yourself properly or qualifying your remarks	???

When someone disagrees with you, not yielding to his/her point of view flatly and saying no more.   ???

Supporting another person's comment when you do agree, rather than keeping silent.   ???

You'll notice that in the list above, all the American responses are qualified by saying you should do so "politely" or "properly." This is a key point. Being direct, disagreeing, arguing your position, interjecting your feelings must all be done appropriately for the American style of discourse. This is not necessarily easy to accomplish, and must be learned and practiced. One very effective technique that can be practiced throughout the day in almost any situation is called "mirroring."

Mirroring

Before you even fully understand what underlying principles are at work, an extremely helpful way to improve your American style of expression is by "mirroring." With this technique you would consciously observe others around you and subtly "mirror" or copy their demeanor, gestures and expressive style.

Social scientists report that all people, from all cultures, do this naturally to some extent. We all have observed husbands and wives who not only sound and act alike, but even start to resemble one another after many years of marriage.

This is true of some research or business sales team members or others who have worked and talked closely together for a long period of time. In fact, videotaped studies have shown that when we become truly engaged in a sympathetic conversation with others, people tend to fall into the communication pattern of the dominant member of the group. There is a subtle adjustment during the conversation, until finally everyone involved adopts certain common gestures, verbal expressions, and phrasing.

Novice ESL students are often told to listen to actors, newscasters and clear-speaking teachers to hear English spoken with proper pronunciation and intonation. They are encouraged to watch such clear speakers on TV or streaming online, and then in the privacy of their homes to mimic the mouth positions they see on the screen.

In all these forms, "mirroring" is at work. Even without further understanding "why" you should express yourself one way or another, you can routinely start to observe and mirror the style of those you admire and wish to emulate or impress.

As you "mirror" you will begin to see what style is effective and appropriate for the region and culture of your particular industry or academic discipline. You will observe, for example, acceptable patterns for interrupting, confronting, disagreeing, adding substance or detail, and concluding your remarks.

Specific Applications & Softening Your Style

Now to examine specific situations you will want to understand and practice, remember that you should always communicate underlying respect for the other person and his/her point of view. You do this by softening your tone and content in just the first few phrases. Going on too long comes off as hypocrisy or empty flattery, which are unattractive qualities in American culture.

Let's look at some phrases and non-verbal ways to "soften" the effect you want to make, while still allowing you to speak assertively and command respect and attention from your listeners.

Smooth Engaging ("polite interrupting)

A full discussion of this—including cultural perceptions of "interrupting" and ways to "jump in" smoothly—were discussed in detail in the previous chapter on Non-Verbal Communication, under the section called *Signaling and Interrupting to Enter a Conversation*.

But in addition to the non-verbal clues that show your desire to join the discourse, you can add verbal phrases to announce your intentions.

Let me say one thing here, please...

If I may, there's an important consideration here....

Sorry to interrupt but...

One second before we go on...

Just to clarify for a minute...

Sorry, but I need to mention....

The phrases should be short and introductory, rather than substantive. Launching directly into a long comment *would* seem like impolite interrupting. Without a strongly voiced but appropriately humble and brief "lead-in," you could be perceived as trying to take over completely.

At the same time, the lead-in remarks are exactly that, entrees to the remarks you want to make in detail. You need first to signal your intention to speak, and only then, when you are noticed (and "have the basketball"), can you add your meaningful content.

Softening Your Direct Talk (being "politely direct")

In the next chapter, you will see in detail how Americans are uniquely direct among speakers throughout the world when framing their arguments and presenting their ideas and positions on an issue. True, there are other cultures (remember Boris and Igor) where certain kinds of remarks can be very direct, too, but there is a difference.

Yes, Americans will present their point of view clearly at the outset, without repetition, before offering substantive elaboration, and unobscured by tangential information. But still, like all forms of conversation, it may be softened with lead-in remarks that allow the speaker to relate amicably with others before stating the content directly. Only after a pleasant personal connection is implied will the speaker proceed to interject comments, disagree, or otherwise express his/her own opinion quite directly.

I hope this doesn't come off as too argumentative, but I think we need to ask...

Maybe I misunderstand what you're saying, but my concern is...

Sorry, but do you mean that...

You may have considered this, but why...

Certainly I have not worked on this project for long, but I'm wondering if...

Disagreeing "Agreeably"

This is simply a variation of being direct; your goal is still to show respect for the other person and his/her point of view while disagreeing with it. Again, you do this by softening your tone and content in just the first few phrases, and adding appropriate non-verbal gestures. And only then, do you state your argument.

I can see all the work you've put into this, but I have to say...

Of course you may be completely right, John, but I think we would all feel 100% confident if we ran one more test and clarified the question...

Maybe I misunderstand what you're saying, but why shouldn't we consider...

Seems like you've thought of just about everything, but have you considered significant differences in the West Coast market...

Tremendous job, clearly, but I feel there are possibly two areas yet to be worked on...

Agreeing "Substantively" (using specifics)

With team efforts or in the decision-making process, it is often useful to verbalize your agreement. Sitting silently is no substitute for stating your position with a new twist, even if the general point has already been eloquently and persuasively expressed.

But simply saying "I agree" is too curt. Instead, take this opportunity to express yourself as a competent, engaged player. Show your ability to reinforce another's argument in well-spoken English, and at the same time connect with your colleagues.

Be specific and substantive when you endorse an idea. Instead of using lengthy generalities, be **specific and substantive**. This is your chance to extend the original argument and speak knowledgeably.

> *I couldn't agree more,* **particularly with Fred's plan to stretch the rollout over two years.** *That way we can...*

> *I endorse the idea completely.* **This way, we should see profits in the near term, which after all is a priority...**

> *I like it!* **Not only do we...but we also can...**

> *Terrific idea.* **I especially like the way you've...**

Finishing Your Point – Not Allowing Others to Interrupt Too Soon

Americans may try to cut short your presentation of an idea by interrupting boldly. This may happen for any of several reasons:

1. They may be competitive and rudely want to steal your command at this moment;

2. They may feel you are going on too long (which is possible) and they want to get directly to the point; or

3. They may think you're finished when in fact you are not.

While maintaining a cordial and open facial expression and relaxed demeanor, you can still use some firm expression to regain your place as speaker. The method here is *"Disarm and Take Back."*

One second, George, let me finish one small point. (Then keep your remarks direct and concise, in case in fact you are rambling and losing your listeners' attention).

Before you start, Peter, I have a little more to say, if you don't mind.

Jim, before we move on, I would feel better if we could briefly talk about how we can fund the effort.

Qualifying or Explaining Your Remarks

Sometimes you may get push-back or disagreement from others after you've expressed an idea. Instead of attacking your attacker, create accommodation and keep the lines of communication cordial. Do this with soft lead-in's, not direct rebuttal.

Re-state the objection to disarm the offensive posture: *Mike, I think I see why you're objecting. You're concerned about the number of man-hours needed to get through Phase One, so let me explain how we can deal with that...*

Blame yourself (not your opponent) for the disagreement, thereby gaining another chance to make your case: *I think I haven't explained this clearly. Let me put it another way...*

Accommodate the other point of view and then bring the discussion back to your ideas: *That's a great point, Karen. I think we could easily adopt your plan by....and then still continue to reap the benefits of .....in my proposal.*

Flatter your opponent's efforts, but stick to your convictions: *I love your way of looking at problems because you are never impractical, but in this case I truly believe we have to focus on...*

In all situations the goal is the same: keep communication open, friendly and connected, and moving in the direction you want. Maintaining this position, mentally and physically, will make others want to work with you, impress your superiors with your ability to both follow and lead, and improve your working life in a new American environment.

CHAPTER SIX

Presenting & Defending Your Ideas

Why don't they appreciate my contributions?

Apart from clear pronunciation, appropriate gestures and body language, and an appealing personality behind your words, a complex message or explanation can be lost if it is not *framed* in the proper way for the American listener.

Knowing how to present concepts in ways that connect with the American pattern of understanding is an important talent very much worth cultivating.

Americans React to You

American middle-manager working for foreign automaker in the U.S., commenting on the outside boss brought in to train local supervisors: *He tries to motivate us and instill some sort of foreign work ethic, but he can't explain what he wants or why this approach is better than what we are used to. We ask for clarification, and he looks at us as if to say, "What's wrong with you that you can't understand this simple idea?"*

So I stopped asking. Now he thinks I get it and I'm with him, but I'm not. I'm totally lost. Bad situation when the boss and the team can't get on the same page!

American member of R&D team headed by non-native manager: *Oh, the endless meetings! She talks and talks, giving us more background than we need, talking down to us, expounding on her past successes –why? to impress us?— and citing other examples that have no real bearing on what we're talking about. And then, after our eyes have glazed over she says a word or two about what she wants, and we almost miss it!*

American academic colleague at international symposium: *I know we're supposed to be doing cutting edge field work together, but it doesn't have to be presented in such an obscure, roundabout way. Just because he's originally from the country that pioneered this work doesn't mean we have to defer to this arrogant guy.*

American patient commenting on her non-native medical doctor: *He doesn't talk to me. He's just so clinical and impersonal. He examines me in silence, orders tests, and announces his diagnosis in few* *words. I ask more questions, and he blurts out short, vague answers. "Yes, no, not really, it's hard to say, we'll know more later," and the one I hate most, "It's complicated; trust me on this."*

I don't know if this means he doesn't believe I have a brain or the right to know about my own health. Or maybe he just doesn't have time for me. It's possible he's merely a cold, indifferent, cavalier kind of guy. Then again, he may simply not have the words!

Presenting and Defending Your Ideas

In your daily work you will frequently ask a question, offer a clarifying answer, try to persuade or prove a point, or even deliver an entire presentation. But often your insights go unappreciated.

As you begin to speak, you know you have something important to say, are thoughtful and prepared, and are standing up bravely to express your ideas. And then, to your surprise, you discover that you have lost your listeners, either because they've tuned you out or they seem confused. One way or another, no one "gets it." How and why could this be?

Linguists and business school professors have long struggled to understand the basis for this *clarity deficit*. As far back as the late 1960's this problem was explored as it related to writing ("Cultural Thought Patterns in Inter-Cultural Education," by Robert B. Kaplan, from *Language Learning 16*, Blackwell Publishers, 1966). Kaplan, and in succeeding decades many other notable linguists, developed a range of theories about patterns of communication among second language learners. They agreed that communication patterns varied according to one's native culture.

The fundamentals of such findings, I believe, apply directly to the problem you are having when you open your mouth to speak at work. I am convinced, after long experience coaching non-native professionals to present and defend their ideas more effectively, that remarkable improvement is possible if you understand the ramifications of Kaplan's original theory.

So *various cultures conceptualize ideas in different ways, and the educational systems of those cultures further reinforce this practice.*

That is, **people mentally formulate ideas in unique, culture-specific patterns and then express those thoughts accordingly.**

The following diagram, originally suggested in Kaplan's 1966 work, illustrates the thinking process that leads to a speaker's making a point (indicated by the arrow in each case).

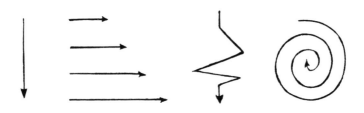

Figure 15 (left-right: American, Semitic, European, and Oriental thought patterns)

Consider first **the American pattern** as you contrast it with others. It is a simple straight-lined arrow. The point is made directly and clearly, without repetition or introductory elaboration.

- Semitic cultures may view such naked directness as un-assertive and vague, because there is no repetitive reinforcement;

- Europeans may see the American pattern as uneducated and self-centered, lacking any scholarly references or deference first to other people, history, or schools of thought; and

- Some Oriental cultures may feel Americans express themselves rudely and abruptly, lacking artfully polite introductory comments, or they may see Americans as "talking-down" and paternalistic, because the expression leads you along step by step and gives no credit to the listener, who can make his/her own connections.

Consider what happens, then, when this American pattern comes into play with a contrasting pattern.

First, **the Semitic zigzag pattern** --often attributed to the cultures of Arabic, Farsi and Hebrew speakers, and others in the Middle East:

> An American tourist is in a Middle Eastern souk or marketplace. The tourist is approached by a rug merchant.
>
> *"Hey sir, want to buy a beautiful rug?* (The American waves him off. The merchant pursues the tourist.)
>
> *"Just take a look, beautiful rug."* (Tourist says a simple "No thanks." Merchant pursues.) *"Fine hand work here, no machines."* (Tourist is annoyed. "No, thank you!")
>
> *"I give you special price. How much you can pay?"*

At this point, the merchant is satisfied he has begun to make a respectable sales pitch. He has not even heard the tourist's refusal.

Only now, the angered American ramps up his response. The American stops walking, looks directly at the merchant and says, *"No thank you! I do not want to buy a rug today. I can't take it back with me. I don't have time right now. Plus, I don't have money for this, at any price. And anyway, there's no space in my house for a rug. So please, no thanks!"*

ONLY NOW DOES THE MERCHANT HEAR AND ACCEPT THE TOURIST'S REFUSAL.

In both cases, the zigzag pattern is finally clear. Statements needed to be repeated, each time with more conviction, in order for them to be communicated. And the American has come away very annoyed.

The European Model exists even beyond the Continent, in many areas of the Western and former colonial world where a European educational system has been influential.

A European-American joint venture is debating whether to allocate money to repair an existing bridge spanning the European city, or build a completely new one. At a meeting, the chairman asks for a voice-vote on which way to proceed.

An American begins: *I say build a completely new bridge. We have the know-how and the budget, and it will make an impressive, bold statement.*

Next, a European speaks: *Europe has a history, of course, of bridges, since its cities are so often bisected by rivers. In our small country alone, there are no fewer than six important waterways that are crucial to transport, to say nothing of social cohesion...*

You may recall that in the 12th century, Frederick I famously said that the empire's success was directly commensurate with its greater number of strong bridges relative to those of its enemies...

There's no question that we Europeans believe that preservation has almost a moral –and certainly aesthetic—quality that warrants its acceptance...

Our engineers will tell you that they routinely prefer renovation over destruction and re-creation. We have learned how to achieve results without financial hardship. That may be different from the American experience, but it is something we proudly hold on to...

Considering all this, I vote for repair and renovation.

Thus, the American has employed his direct pattern, stating first his point (*build a new bridge*) and then briefly supporting that argument with direct reasons why. By contrast, the European must first show that he is both intellectually worthy and broadly knowledgeable enough to express an opinion. So the line to his point digresses along the way. He cites history, statistics (*no fewer than six bridges*), the words of celebrated people, philosophy (morals and aesthetics), common current practice, and financial considerations, to name a few!

Meanwhile, the American reacts negatively: he is bored and annoyed by so much talk, and he feels the European is showing off, impolite, arrogant and insufferably long-winded.

With **the Latin variant of the European model**, politeness and flowery lead-in's often preface comments. Before the point is made, the speaker moves from preliminary comment to preliminary comment, and at each change of direction the speaker states some personal expression of consideration (*if I'm not disturbing you, I'd like to ask; ...and tell me first, how are the kids? I heard they were home sick yesterday; ...oh, and by the way, did you enjoy the weekend with your Chilean visitors; etc.*)

The Russian variant would look like a dotted line replacing the otherwise European pattern, indicating an unsmooth, disjointed flow of conversation. Combined with the frequent omission of articles by Russian speakers in English, the impression to Americans is one of halting, disconnected, not thoroughly thought out speech.

> *Solution to problem is sketchy. You need details. Timeframe. Cost. Who's on the team. Is there leader or all work together? You need direction. Cannot be too many cooks..."spoil the soup," as you say.*

The American has to pay close attention to mentally fill in the gaps as an idea unfolds. The simple addition of connecting adverbs and conjunctions (*so that, in order to, consequently, instead of, as a result, on the contrary,* etc.) largely eliminates the problem.

> *In order to find a solution, we need sufficient details. For instance, what's the timeframe? How about the cost? And most important, with regard to the team, who's on it and who leads it?*

I say we need a leader who knows how to give direction, since collaboration alone doesn't get the job done. At worst, it wastes time and money, and consequently results in failure all around.

The spiral Oriental pattern is particularly evident in Japan, less so in Korea, and it exists in the "soft-spoken" cultures of Southeast Asia, as well.

After an initial meeting with an American company, a potential Japanese client returns to Japan. The Americans want to follow up with a visit to Tokyo to continue talks, and so they propose a 2-day meeting in April.

American: *"So, would sometime the week of April 9th work for you?"*

Japanese: *"Ah, April is cherry blossom time in Japan. Our company leaves work to go outside to enjoy the cherry blossoms together, this year April 11 and 12. Our working group is one family in this special time... The United States visit was very good. We enjoyed our talks. Continuing is good for both of us...Kyoto is the best place for viewing in April, a one day trip from Tokyo. We are honored to show you. We are happy for this good relationship!"*

The American then wonders to himself, *So is that a yes? Should we book the flight and the hotel? For exactly when? Should we allow more than 2 days, since maybe they're suggesting Kyoto? Would that be Kyoto and Tokyo?*

The spiral pattern is at work here, winding thoughts together without any clear progression for the American mind. The conversation moves almost poetically, and the point –the answer to the American's initial question—is obscure. Reading between the lines is challenging!

Applying the American Pattern to All Communication

If you attended a U.S. school or university at some point in your life, you may have seen how Americans are taught to write a "proper paragraph." It includes a "topic sentence" or "thesis statement," followed by supporting information. Beginning with concise wording of the main point you want to make, you then move to a detailed defense of that point, either later in the paragraph or in succeeding paragraphs.

In exactly the same way, Americans routinely employ this "outline form" when speaking, and have always been encouraged by American teachers to present arguments or facts in this form.

And that is now how you must delineate your ideas. In fact, the full playout of your idea or concept could be illustrated precisely by turning the European pattern upside down, so that you would begin with your point (arrow) and then diverge into relevant, supporting details. *In all your business communication, this is the pattern that should be evident.*

Handling Q & A's

Providing answers or explanations of any kind –whether in one-on-one conversations, meetings, or larger forums, including follow-ups of your own presentations—is always the same:

- if necessary, *disarm* to make your "opponent" more receptive;

- then *directly answer* the stated question;

- finally, *add detail (elaboration)* or explain how/why/etc. in an ordered way.

Here is a response to a question about a pharmaceutical product currently under development.

> Q: *Why do you feel we should present our findings now, when we still have two trials to complete before being ready to go to market?*

> A: **Disarm:***That's a valid concern, no question, but I believe there is one overriding factor that we cannot overlook.* **Direct answer:** *Our biggest competitor is scheduled to launch its competing product in two weeks. If we miss this window to announce our product at the same time, our eventual news will be "old news."* **1st elaboration:** *I say let the public's mind keep us at the forefront, and they will forever more connect us with the remedy.* **2nd elaboration:** *Remember two years ago we were in the same position with XYZ. We waited, and we lost out.*

Here is another Q. and A. example from an auto dealership:

> Q: *How can you possibly say we should push certified pre-owned vehicles when we need to move the more profitable new models!*

A. Disarm: *You're absolutely right that we have to be concerned about the bottom line, and normally new models are the way to go, but* **Direct answer**: *recently I've seen two new factors at work that say the opposite.* **1ˢᵗ elaboration**: *First, the economy is not what it was even six months ago –and it shows no signs of improving any time soon – so if we're pushing only new cars, our models are out of reach for a big segment of the market.* **2ⁿᵈ elaboration**: *And second, I've seen too many people lately come in, check the sticker price and walk away. If I can hold them by promoting the pre-owned car, that's a sale we otherwise would not have at all.*

Framing a Longer Presentation

The same format applies to presentations or lead-in's to any longer explanation:

- First *create a friendly, open connection* with your audience. Establish a relationship that will be warm and receptive.

- Then *state your central theme*, the point they should keep in mind and apply to everything that will be discussed.

- After that, *proceed with the details* of your presentation, always connecting to the core idea.

Here are excerpts from a presentation on state-of-the art web design.

Establish a positive relationship: I've seen some spectacular – truly spectacular—websites created over the last five years. And I recognize some of you here today who I know were among the most innovative designers out there. Real game-changers. At the time I thought our industry could hardly improve on that great work.

Transition to central theme: *But in fact, that was then, and this is now. Five years is an eternity in our business, and the reality today is* **Central Theme:** *we no longer lead, we follow! Today our design follows the user! We need to know how and on what devices, apps and search engines the user is getting information, and then design for all those possibilities. We must make sure our platform works and adapts smoothly and precisely to all the devices users employ, not just, say, a single laptop.*

Transition to details: *As we go through this presentation, I will show you the many steps you must consider, in order to create at every level the adaptive environment users expect.*

1st detail: *First, let's take a look at....*

So to summarize, in whatever form your comments, concerns, ideas, or explanations take, remember to employ American directness as your communication model. After connecting on a personal level, as described in chapter 3, move directly to your point. State it succinctly and clearly, and then in a systematic way, run down the various reasons, examples, statistics or other supporting comments that reinforce your main point. At the end, you may wish to reiterate the central point again.

And remember the ever-popular American "outline" form. As you provide supporting details, verbally list them.

- *"There are three reasons for this. First.... Second is the... And finally..."*

- Or, *"We can separate this into two categories, the practical and the aesthetic. So first, practicality requires that...* (then later) *...And aesthetically, we must acknowledge that..."*

Right or wrong, comfortable for you or not, this is the form your argument must take if you want native listeners to grasp your ideas easily, find what you say stimulating, and enjoy hearing from you. If you are smart (which you are), you will have communicated your competence, and no one will miss that fact!

PART THREE

THE SUCCESSFUL PRESENTATION

Whether you are speaking to a handful of people or before an audience of hundreds, your challenge is the same: you must present a well-developed message clearly and persuasively.

Yet with a full-blown presentation, you invest much more time in preparation. You analyze each element of your talk, note the areas of weakness and improve them, and practice, practice, practice.

This section helps you pull together all that you have learned, and then offers a check-list, lest you overlook some important details.

7. Pulling It All Together

8. Your Personal Comprehensive Checklist

A Celebrity Visitor to America:
Sure to Succeed...if only!

After six years as Minister of Finance, Jorge Manuel Garcia Restrepo (not his real name) had formulated a way to link his country's new economic model for growth with a plan of cooperation with the United States.

And so Garcia set out to present his plan to influential parties in the United States. If he communicated his message clearly, he was certain that worldwide respect and prosperity would be assured for the people of his Latin American nation.

His colleagues encouraged him: who could better represent their country than Garcia? Who knew more about the subject? Who had more connections and respected credentials in the United States, where Garcia had done graduate work years ago.

He would start by speaking to economists and public policy people at a top-tier university. He would then persuade them to open doors for him in Washington.

....

I had worked with many visiting scholars and foreign speakers on American university campuses. I was familiar with the routine of guests being warmly welcomed into the academic community and then quickly thrust into a whirlwind of pre-arranged speaking engagements. From my past experience, I was wary of academic celebrities from outside the U.S. who, because they knew their subject, often overlooked the importance of communicating it properly.

Now here was Minister Garcia, the day after his arrival, moments before his first public lecture. He stood before a 250-seat lecture hall packed with journalists, students, public policy and economics scholars, and anyone else who could squeeze in. Here was a seasoned professional in his world, good looking, not tall but upright and well dressed in a serious tailored suit. After an introduction, Garcia stood behind an imposing lectern, and without notes he began to speak.

Despite a distracting accent, he launched into a fast-paced economic and political history of his country. He addressed the differences between his party's approach and that of its predecessors. He enumerated the steps he'd taken to make changes. He cited statistics. Dispassionately, with neither pride nor fierce persuasion, he urged support to continue and expand his policies.

Reminded that he was running long, Garcia closed and announced he would take questions. Many in the hall squirmed and looked for the exit. A few professors expressed lengthy opinions of their own. Minister Garcia's answers were lengthy, as his lecture had been. Most of the audience was quiet or packing to leave, certainly not "fired up."

SUMMARY ANALYSIS: Disappointing first impression because of a fatally flawed delivery in every respect. If only he had realized that:

- **His strong accent, particularly with certain key words, distracted and confused the audience;**

- **By moving around the stage and "freeing himself" from the confines of a too-tall lectern, and by dressing slightly less formally for this audience, he could have cultivated a** less stiff posture and approachable "American" informality, and connected better with his audience;

- By not following the direct American style of organization, he "bored" his audience with meandering particulars, instead of stating his point and then proving it with valuable, pertinent details.

- Speaking in a monotone, he failed to take advantage of the power of English intonation to lend power and passion to his key convictions.

- Too proud to use notes, his rambling compromised the clarity of his message and failed to win positive sympathy from his audience.

An opportunity was seriously mishandled, the outcome potentially fatal.

On his first day in America, the visiting speaker would have been wiser to spend a little time shifting into an "American gear" as he adjusted to a different language, culture and communications model.

Had he analyzed *all* aspects of his presentation –beyond the message alone—and then assessed the venue where he would speak, he could have quickly eliminated many of the obstacles to a smooth, clear and persuasive pitch. This would have been relatively easy to achieve. Such preparation would have been time valuably spent.

Pulling It All Together

Before you begin, remember...

You are a competent professional, knowledgeable in your area; otherwise, you would not be making this presentation. But *how* you communicate that competence is always a nagging uncertainty, and that has been the focus of this book. Now—faced with the challenge of taking the stage and performing before an audience you need to impress—you must pull together all the elements that contribute to a successful talk.

Of course, you must have something to say and a point of view about the subject. Further, you will have a goal to achieve, whether to educate your audience, bring them around to your way of thinking, produce a desired action or outcome as a result, or all of the above.

You have worked to become technically savvy, and through practice you can nimbly negotiate the aids –Smartboard, PowerPoint, props or other demonstration equipment—you will need while speaking. Yet through it all, your most challenging task will be to *communicate* properly, to *connect* with your audience as you speak. From the outset, your listeners must be drawn to you and feel that your message is worthy of their interest and attention. Losing sight of this all-important objective can destroy an otherwise spectacular message.

So in preparing to make the right first impression, analyze and separate your talk into distinct communications areas, as discussed in this book, chapter by chapter, including:

- verbal precision and control,

- non-verbal gestures and other techniques for connecting with an American audience, and

- building your message in a style that fits a typical American's thought patterns and is comfortable for *them.*

And finally, rehearse until you can deliver the presentation smoothly and automatically.

Let's review some key points to hold in the forefront of your presentation planning.

- *Speak clearly.* Part One will help you analyze your accent and then determine what warrants the most preparation and practice, and then attention upon delivery. From Chapter 1 (*Fixing Your Accent Where It Matters*), see which sounds merit your attention. Then in Chapter 2 (*Your Troublesome Consonants and Vowels*), review the practice exercises that help you to eliminate those patterns and tendencies from your first language that cause confusion for your American listeners in English.

- *Speak deliberately*, that is, with a careful, slower pace, adjusted to emphasize key words. Along with verbal clarity, employing the "music" of American English, as explained in Chapter 3, will greatly reduce the stress level of your audience, enabling them to sit back and comfortably focus on your presentation.

- As you move around the speaking area --manipulating a Smartboard, performing a physical demonstration, or otherwise shifting from being still to getting up or moving—*be aware of your body language*. Within Part Two, Chapter 4 reminds you of the non-verbal messages your physical stance projects, and helps you communicate an image of relaxed confidence and knowledge about your message.

- *Connect with your audience as people –American* people or others used to that style of communication. From Part Two, Chapters 4 (*When Gestures Speak Louder Than Words*) and 5 (*Connecting with People "American Style"*) will remind you of both overt and subtle, unspoken ways to achieve this.

  Because after all, *connecting is critical to building an image of trust for yourself and your message.* And being seen as "trustworthy" allows you to convince others of your value and knowledge. Trust makes them want what *you* want. Trust is the essence of winning.

- And finally, *analyze your technique*: *how* you state what you know, *how* you defend your message, and *how* you organize your ideas to be in sync with the organizational mindset of your audience. Make the required critical cultural adjustments on your part. Look again at Chapter 6.

And then, after your successful presentation is delivered, start building a Personal Checklist over time, so that you can self-monitor for future speaking opportunities. The next and final chapter will help you get started.

Your Personal Comprehensive Checklist

People don't fall asleep during conversations, but they do at presentations! Nancy Duarte wisely pointed this out in her HBR Guide to *Persuasive Presentations* (Harvard Business Review Publishing Corporation, 2012).

And what accounts for the difference? Why can a conversation be a pleasure, while a presentation more of a chore?

The answer is simple: people find a conversation appealing because they are engaged with one another and with what each says and thinks during its course. There is a back-and-forth process, between the utterance of one person and the active, interested processing of that message by the other. Essentially, *a good conversation involves a good* **connection** *between people.*

> No matter how formal or serious your presentation may be, it can have the appeal of a conversation if you incorporate the notion of "connection" into every aspect of its delivery.

"Connection" has been a central theme throughout this book, since it is the essence of successful communication. Aware of it or not, you are constantly sending messages, impressions and signals to your audience about:

- the value of your talk before it even starts
- yourself, before you utter a word
- whether you really *know* your subject
- whether you will present your material in an easy-to-absorb way, or not
- whether your presentation will be beneficial or a waste of time
- whether the audience may be in the presence of a rising star (you!).

Here then is a summary of suggestions to help you build a Personal Comprehensive Checklist when faced with the challenge of your next presentation.

ADVANCE WORK

First impressions are lasting impressions.

Before your talk begins, think about the overall impression your audience receives when they first walk into the room, when they initially enter the space, feel the ambience, and observe you from a distance. What your audience sees in these first moments can set the tone and predispose them to receive you either positively or skeptically. So for example:

1. Proper Preparation for a Good First Impression

- Have you confirmed in advance that you will have:
  - ✓ the proper size room for your audience (not so big that the presentation seems under-attended, and not so small that the event will feel overcrowded),
  - ✓ adequate seating,
  - ✓ a sound system working well,
  - ✓ comfortable temperature control,
  - ✓ no interruptions. So that your audience isn't disturbed once the presentation has started, find ways in advance to encourage prompt arrival (or seating in a separate section for latecomers), announce when breaks will be taken, explain your plan for taking questions, etc.

- Are you prepared and organized with:
  - ✓ notes in order,
  - ✓ laptop or other devices connected and ready,
  - ✓ audio-visual devices properly set up, and
  - ✓ hand-outs graphically pleasing and in sufficient quantity, and a plan for easy distribution?

- Have you practiced maintaining "professional balance" by being:
    - ✓ relaxed, friendly and comfortable with your *audience*, yet
    - ✓ serious and knowledgeable about your *subject*?
- Will you respect your audience by:
    - ✓ starting and finishing on time?

MAKING YOUR FIRST APPEARANCE

Your audience may observe you before the official presentation, perhaps as you check your visual aids, plug in your laptop, chat informally with others, sort through notes, or sit alone.

Throughout the presentation and, for that matter, throughout your career, you must never try to be something you are not. Always be yourself, but *within your authentic and competent identity, still remember always to project a sense of relaxed confidence in who you are.*

So even though, for instance, you are a thorough person who methodically checks and re-checks your equipment, do this in a seemingly effortless way. Look and act professional as you move smoothly through the steps you will follow, with a controlled demeanor at all times.

Or if you arrive early and must wait nervously for the talk to begin, exhibit positive, open body language. In particular, project a confident posture and an engaging, contentedly smiling face. Periodically look outward, scanning the crowd, or even briefly acknowledging from a distance someone you may recognize. In other words, look like someone whom others would feel comfortable approaching at a party.

This is the moment when the audience will form first impressions and become predisposed, right or wrong, about what to expect from you. So here's the second part of your checklist.

2. Present a Positive Image and an Engaging Demeanor

✓ Always be yourself…but always a prepared, controlled, confident version of that authentic self.

✓ From Part Two, review all the ways you can project your competence *in a relaxed, outgoing and confident* way. Chapter 3 will cover non-verbal gestures and expressions and Chapter 4 about how to "connect" with people.

✓ Keep a positive focus on *you*, not on what you're wearing. Your clothing should not be a distracting fashion statement, nor should it send a negative image by being rumpled or otherwise unkempt. Everything about you should look carefully prepared and reflect suitably on your message.

✓ Dress with the seriousness of a presenter, but appropriately and not too formally for your audience.

✓ Women in particular should avoid visual distractions, such as dangling earrings or flashy jewelry, very immodest necklines, sleeveless tops, very short skirts, uncomfortable looking heels, etc.

✓ Be "body aware." Sense your body in relation to your audience and your visual exhibits, trying to stay connected with the audience with a direct line between your face and theirs. Try not to put your back to them for any length of time when, for example, calling attention to a particular slide.

✓ Keep an open, expansive appearance that suggests confidence, rather than a constricted or contrived one that projects insecurity and insincerity. Avoid "closing your stance" by crossing your arms or legs, clasping your hands tightly or putting them both in your pockets.

✓ Standing or sitting, maintain an upright but not stiff posture.

✓ Exhibit "controlled energy" to convey both a deliberate pace of speaking yet an enthusiastic visual alertness.

✓ Avoid moving your arms or hands excessively and to no effect. Holding a laser pointer, remote control, white board marker, etc. in one or both hands in front of you can help.

✓ In front of a big audience in a large venue, however, you may want to exaggerate your movements, but do so only to effect, not nervously at random.

✓ Share eye contact with all your audience, not limiting it to one listener or one part of the room.

✓ Employ facial gestures to complement your verbal expression: smiles, eyebrow raising, nodding, etc. at appropriate moments. Move your head naturally, and move your relaxed facial muscles.

AND NOW YOU SPEAK

3. Vocal Elements

How you speak is just as important as *what* you say. Your brilliant ideas cannot be communicated without a clear, strong verbal delivery.

✓ Review Chapter One to identify your first language's special pronunciation challenges.

✓ Pronounce clearly and correctly, especially enunciating your consonants at the ends of words.

✓ Say your presentation's key terms clearly (practice a list of these in advance).

✓ Enunciate fully and visibly. Open your mouth and move your lips actively. Make sure your mouth and lips are visible to your audience, if possible.

✓ Speak with power, not running out of breath at the end of your sentences. Maintain good, upright chest posture while talking.

✓ Speak with vocal variety and not in a monotone (doing the former makes you seem passionate and engaged; doing the latter is guaranteed to bore your audience). Stress and stretch out key words. Hold your "point" a little longer, dropping your tone downward.

✓ Control your pace. Don't speak too fast. In your presentation, speak slower than you would in a normal conversation. Add pauses around key points and key words.

✓ Even though you are an advanced speaker of English, watch your grammar. Remind yourself of those words and expressions that catch you up because they are different in your first language.

For example, "people" and many other such words is a *plural* noun in American English but *singular* in many other languages, so be sure your verb is in agreement. The converse is also true: words like *information, equipment, advice* and others are singular in English but often plural in other languages. So remember to say, "Many people *think* that my advice *is* good.

Also remember particles, those little words that follow certain verb expressions which may also vary in your first language. For example, "She is married *to* (not *with*) my brother."

4. Winning Over Your Audience as You Begin to Speak

✓ Start with a humanizing, "connecting" opening remark, thanking your introducer with relaxed style, and acknowledging your audience in a friendly way.

✓ Be careful about attempts at humor. Opening with an amusing story or comment is a frequent suggestion for public speakers in general, but for non-native speakers, humor can be dangerous territory! Jokes definitely do not translate easily from one culture to another. The audience may respond with blank or confused faces, and you then can become flustered at their reaction. Best to avoid.

✓ A more certain way to connect with your audience and build trust is by letting your non-verbal gestures, your facial connections, your incidental remarks, and your relaxed demeanor establish your comfort level with both the audience and your subject.

5. Communicating with Visual Aids

Visual aids are an important part of your presentation, and another valid form of communication. This area must be as practiced and professional as your personal delivery is.

✓ Still, remember that *you* are the presenter, not your slides. The slide will signal information, but *you* must explain it with your own words.

✓ Even though you may want to expand upon it, *a slide should be understandable without any accompanying talk.* Keep the words on the slide brief and limited.

✓ *Do not read your slides*; doing this suggests you need the projected image to help you know what to say. You do not want the audience to infer that you can't express yourself easily, that you have nothing more add, that you cannot be a spontaneous speaker…basically, that you are not facile and fluent with your subject.

✓ Enhance your slides with your own words of clarification, further explanation, examples, or relevant real-life anecdotes.

✓ Depending on the size of the audience and your presentation space, it may be better to *present your slides from your laptop and use a laser pointer* to draw attention to elements under discussion. In smaller situations, however, you may prefer to walk to the screen (as long as you don't cover it), in order to keep yourself connected with the audience's line of sight.

✓ Either way, *do not put your back to the audience.* Face your listeners whenever you talk, glancing up at the slide or down at your laptop only for a quick moment if necessary.

MAKING YOUR PITCH

6. **Delivering an American-style Message**

✓ Review Chapter Four and remember the all-important American pattern for communicating ideas.

- Open with a concise, clear statement of your central theme, what you hope to demonstrate overall, and the point they should keep in mind and apply to everything that will be discussed.

- Offer a brief rundown of how your presentation will go, what steps you will follow, when you will take questions, and assurances that the audience should should seek clarification if anything is confusing or unclear as you go along, etc.

- With visual aids, proceed in the promised order. If you want to repeat a slide to aid recall, repeat it; *don't* go back and run the risk of problems adjusting your technology.

✓ *Anticipate* resistances or points of confusion, and address them as they come up.

✓ Stay focused on your central theme, and tie any ancillary comments or diversions back to your main premise. Don't give any reason for the audience to wonder if you're wandering off-message.

7. Engaging with Your Audience from Beginning to End

Everything about your presentation must convey a desire to care for and engage with your audience. In a way, you should assume the role of a good host, authentically introducing yourself, making them comfortable, and then saying something of interest that they will want to listen to.

✓ Make your presentation seem collaborative, not like a "canned speech." Draw the audience in by your natural manner, including:

- Your choice of words, using shorter over longer ones, and single words over longer expressions ("Because he's a brilliant scientist" works better than "The fact that he is a man of great intelligence in his field of science…")

- Avoid stilted jargon ("really" is better than "in point of fact"; "50-50" is better than "six of one and half a dozen of the other").

- Limit the impersonal-sounding passive voice (instead of saying, "It is felt by many experts in the field…"; say, "Many experts feel…").

✓ Be approachable by sounding modest, not arrogant. Let your audience draw their own conclusions about your brilliance from the message itself.

✓ Be passionate and energized about your subject. Be joyous, not somber. Interject excitement as you speak, or little asides to the audience like, "And so we can see here –*and this is something I really love about the product*—that…"

✓ Bring your slides and other visuals to life. *Don't read them* (the audience can do that without you); instead, *expand upon them* with paraphrased explanations, anecdotes proving a point, stories bring the message home, etc.

And keep the verbiage brief and limited on those slides, allowing them to enhance or illustrate what *you* are talking about, not the other way around.

✓ If you choose to personalize a point by telling a little story, draw the audience into your experience. Make it come alive with evocative words, realistic and sensory images, and gestures and facial expressions that suggest you are still in the moment.

FOLLOW UP

8.   Closing the Presentation with Questions and Answers

You should decide whether you want to take questions throughout the presentation, or at the end, and announce that fact. Doing the former takes more practice, as it may throw off your timing or even, in worst cases, cause you to cede control of your subject to a questioner. Announcing in the beginning that you wish to hold questions until the end, still allows you to be truly "in conversation" with your audience. Either way, remember:

✓ *Anticipate* what questions may be asked, and practice your response. That way you won't be caught searching for an answer.

✓ *Listen carefully* to the question, to be sure you understand the questioner's area of confusion. If you're too quick to jump into your prepared answer, you may miss the actual sub-text of the question, that is, what the questioner really wants to know.

✓ *If you don't know the answer, say so.* Then maybe explore the question with the audience, explain why the answer is not known, describe what yet needs to be done to arrive at an answer, or suggest another mode of followup.

✓ *When time is up, come to a controlled close* instead of an abrupt stop. Finish with a final strong, summarizing message line. Send your audience off with something to remember and something to contemplate into the future.

Add to this Comprehensive Personal Checklist as your own situation warrants. And be sure to practice all these points well before your presentation.

Engage the help of one or more colleagues or friends, preferably native speakers, to watch you rehearse your presentation. Have them prepare for their role by first reading this summary, and then they can judge whether you have successfully addressed all these important areas.

And When It's Over...

When the presentation has been delivered...when you've finished reading this book...when it's over...

Well, in fact it's *never* over. You will want to refresh your communications techniques throughout your career and throughout your life in North America. You will surely succeed professionally and continue to progress the longer you remain in the American workplace.

But reminding yourself of key communications pointers should be an ongoing task, keeping your presentations always fresh and you always at the top of your game.

You have always been a bright, talented and dedicated professional. Yet no matter how proficient you were in your field of knowledge, many times in the past you delivered unclear or unhelpful messages while trying to convey that knowledge.

Now you know how to take command of your communication with clearer pronunciation and verbal delivery, a discrete choice of word expressions, subtle shifts in body language, and an understanding of culturally and situationally appropriate ways of relating to others.

Now you can fully communicate your competence in order to:

- earn a job promotion or a raise or a chance to lead
- prove to teammates that you are a valuable asset
- make friends and win trust among colleagues and clients
- help others to appreciate your insights and good ideas

- reveal to the world that you are a rising star worth watching!

Congratulations on your progress. You deserve your success at every level!

INDEX